Arthur H. Barrington

Anti-Christian Cults

An attempt to show that spiritualism, theosophy, and Christian science are devoid

of supernatural powers and are contrary to the Christian religion

Arthur H. Barrington

Anti-Christian Cults
An attempt to show that spiritualism, theosophy, and Christian science are devoid of supernatural powers and are contrary to the Christian religion

ISBN/EAN: 9783337042189

Printed in Europe, USA, Canada, Australia, Japan

Cover: Foto ©Lupo / pixelio.de

More available books at **www.hansebooks.com**

Anti=Christian Cults.

AN ATTEMPT TO SHOW THAT

Spiritualism, Theosophy and Christian Science

ARE DEVOID OF SUPERNATURAL POWERS AND
ARE CONTRARY TO THE CHRISTIAN RELIGION.

—BY—

A. H. BARRINGTON, A.B., B.D.,

RECTOR OF CHRIST CHURCH,
JANESVILLE, WIS.

WITH A COMMENDATORY BY
THE BISHOP OF MILWAUKEE.

MILWAUKEE, WIS.:
THE YOUNG CHURCHMAN CO.
LONDON:
SAMPSON LOW, MARSTON & CO.

COPYRIGHT BY
THE YOUNG CHURCHMAN CO.,
1898.

Commendatory.

To the Reader:

THE request to commend this book, coming from a valued Presbyter in this Diocese, and also a dear personal friend, is one to which I very cordially give heed. If only to testify publicly to my warm confidence in him, as a devoted servant of God, in the Ministry of His Church, the request could well be granted.

But beyond this range of personal feeling, one is always glad to commend every honest effort made to stem somewhat, if it may be, this wholesale delusion of the reading public, going on to such a wide extent to-day, by the many clever tricksters, the enchanters, the smooth and easy talkers, the magicians of every degree—great and small—male and female—who come before the public daily with their wares for sale: the new philosophies, their recently patented systems of religion, their fresh panaceas for all our many human ills; and who do thus, in a strange measure, bewitch the public eye; and withal do most egregiously fool the people, lead many weak and unstable Christian folk away from the old faith, aside from the rough and narrow path.

"Cults," these are well called; make-shifts, patent medicine processes; and all thoroughly "Anti-Christian Cults," most veritably and far too effectually, they always prove to be. New they also are, in one sense; and yet not new, in a more true and exact sense. Old and very old, full of decay and moral rottenness; full of foul odors and intellectual poison, and the germs of a fatal spiritual disease hid beneath—as all history well shows. Old ghosts of old-time heresies, they are—each one. Ghosts that will not lie down in their graves; sure to rise again each passing century, or even decade; assume some new and more fanciful dress, perhaps a shade more picturesque and fashionable than before; and so they live again, parading the old lie under changed terms and in smart language; beguiling many weary and sin-laden souls, fooling the people, attracting the unwary, shaking the unstable; as the latest fashions, the last mental "cult," the newest and freshest "religion" always has done, always will do: something that has come to "reform," to supersede and dethrone the old.

Nor are we at all hopeful or expectant that these innumerable "ghosts" will ever permanently die. Stop them all to-day, and they will all rise up again on the morrow, at least in some other place, and in some other way. "There is nothing new under the sun," not even in these subtle lines of moral and intellectual heresies. And so the long spiritual combat of truth against error, of the Church against the devil, of Christ against Belial, of God against the worldly mammon of unrighteousness, shall ever go on—until "this tyranny be overpast"; and until that bright day of "the new Heavens and the new earth" shall come; when this slow probation of our earthly schooling is done, under the patient discipline of Almighty God; and until His "Fulness of Time" shall be accomplished. We well know Who and What shall win, in that Great Last Day; but we "know not the times or the seasons, which the Father hath placed in His own Power." For this culmination we can only patiently wait, and lovingly "work our work betimes," until that Day shall dawn, and our many earthly shadows shall "flee away."

Yet, let us welcome each and every earnest effort made by every preacher of the old-time Gospel, every lover of the changeless Creed of the passing ages, as he does his share in upholding the Eternal Truth of God, and the Revelation of Jesus Christ; each one standing in his own lot, where his Master may have placed him, narrow though that lot is, modest and humble though his effort may seem to be. Hence, our humble prayer and our affectionate hope is, that the blessing of God may rest upon this book, now issuing from the press, sent out by our dear brother for the helpful reading and the reasonable comfort of his many friends in the Church; and we trust also, for the help of some others who are beyond and without. We well know he sends it out, not for the purpose of controversy, but from a heart and mind full of devotion to the Adorable Person of Jesus Christ our Blessed Lord, "Who of God is made unto us, our Wisdom, our Righteousness, our Sanctification, and our Final Redemption."

ISAAC LEA NICHOLSON,

Milwaukee,   Bishop of Milwaukee.
WHITSUN: 1898.

Author's Preface.

THESE lectures were written for, and delivered before, the parishioners of Christ Church. They are published in the hope that they may enlighten others who are being led astray by Spiritualism, Theosophy, and Christian Science. Sooner or later they must find, to their sorrow, that though there be elements of truth in each of these cults, yet in scope and purpose they are false, subversive of the Christian Faith, and totally unable to afford true comfort and consolation.

Among the many books used in preparation of these lectures, we would specially mention *Earth's Earliest Ages*, by G. H. Pember, M.A., and *Hypnotism*, by Dr. Albert Moll.

Christ Church Rectory,
Janesville, Wis.,
EASTERTIDE, 1898.

Table of Contents.

	PAGE
THE CASE STATED.	11
SPIRITUALISM.	26
SPIRITUALISM. II.	40
THEOSOPHY. I.	66
THEOSOPHY. II.	79
CHRISTIAN SCIENCE. I.	108
CHRISTIAN SCIENCE. II.	133
CONCLUSION.	158

Anti-Christian Cults.

The Case Stated.

WELL spake Rabbi Gamaliel of old when he cautioned the Sanhedrin to "take heed" as to what they intended to do concerning the new faith, which was increasing with such alarming rapidity. "Take heed .... lest haply ye be found even to fight against God." He referred to incidents in the history of the chosen people and then declared: "If this counsel or this work be of men, it will come to nought; but if it be of God ye cannot overthrow it."[1]

---

[1] Acts v. 34-39.

CHRISTIANITY IMPREGNABLE, CHRISTIANS UNSTABLE.

That Christianity is of Divine origin and part of the eternal plan and purpose of the Almighty, we have not the shadow of a doubt. That it can be overthrown, is impossible. We are not, therefore, alarmed about its ultimate success. Nothing could be further from our thoughts. Men do, however, "*fight against God.*" They are timid, and too easily turned from the straight and narrow path. They are readily deceived and to their own hurt. They, like the Athenians of old, are attracted and won over by anything new and strange, till, actually hoping for more light, they are plunged further into darkness. Too many (if there were but two or three, it were too many)—too many are being deceived, and blinded, and led astray to-day, by the false hopes, and promises, and claims of certain religious yet anti-Christian cults which in vain would undermine the truth as it is in Jesus. Undoubtedly, like other fads which spring up in the night of darkness rather than in the light of eternal truth, these shadows of good shall come to nought, as they are unquestionably of men; but, in the meantime, the effect upon the adherents of such substitute religions cannot but be disastrous. History repeats itself and there is no reason to note an exception here. Light and life are found only in the service of Almighty God. To deny Him or to assume to worship Him, while rejecting the light that He has given us, is to plunge into darkness and to invite disaster. Therefore we plead earnestly, lovingly, and in all sincerity, with those who have willingly listened to these false and deceptive ways, to turn from these vanities to serve the living God.

ISRAEL'S PLIGHT.

Gamaliel's counsel was ignored, that the chosen people might "even fight against God." Behold the result! They were looking anxiously forward to the coming of their Messiah, rightly basing all their fondest hopes upon Him, yet when He came they would not accept Him, they could not abide His counsels, but their rejected Messiah is to-day the Christ of history.

It is written: "Cursed is everyone that hangeth on a tree," and the Jews in their desire to heap ignominy upon the hope of all the earth, though His own people, hanged Him to a tree; but behold, the Cross was transformed into the throne of the Lord of lords and King of kings, and Jesus was lifted up thereon, "that whosoever believeth in Him should not perish but have everlasting life."

The Jews consigned their Messiah to the tomb, and from that very moment the glory of Israel faded, while the curse which they would invoke upon their Redeemer has fastened itself upon that people even until now.

Israel sealed her doom at Calvary, yet out of the sepulchre arose "The Light to lighten the Gentiles;" and how the nations, that have seen that great light, have been illuminated; how they have advanced; how they have prospered; how completely have they distanced the nations who are in darkness; how they are still advancing (and that not so much intellectually as morally); all this is due to the preaching of the Gospel, to Christianity; and yet there are those who would give it up for some passing fancy, that can only lead them back into darkness, uncertainty, despair. How many of us realize how very much of the present civilization and enjoyment of life, is directly and solely due to the religion of Jesus Christ?

THE POWER OF CHRIST.

As Dean Alford has said: "That which is most deeply working in modern life and thought is the mind of Christ. His name has passed over our institutions and much more has His Spirit penetrated into our social and domestic existence."

John von Müller, the famous Swiss historian, declares: "Christ is the key to the history of the world. Not only does all harmonize with the mission of Christ; all is subordinated to it."[2]

---

[2] Lorimer's *Argument for Christianity*, 61, 62.

And the great German philosopher, Fichte, says: "We and our whole age are so rooted in the soil of Christianity and have sprung from it; it has exercised its influence in the most manifold ways on the whole of our culture, and we should be absolutely nothing of all that we are, if this mighty principle had not preceded us."

Dr. Lorimer in his admirable work, *The Argument for Christianity*, says: "In France, there is a magnificent cartoon, by Paul Chenavard, representing what may be termed the palingenesis of human society. The great picture is divided into two horizontal zones. In the upper one we have a flaring, noisy, triumphant procession of the imperial Cæsar. There are lictors, generals, banners, spoils, prisoners, elephants, eagles, and indeed everything to suggest insolent and unchallenged power. But the lower zone is pervaded by the feeling of silence, obscurity, patience, and suffering. It discloses the primitive Christians at prayer in the catacombs, which they have dug to serve them both as chapel and grave, beneath the throne of the emperor. The contrast is complete, and like all master-pieces of art, tells its own story. It teaches that the pagan civilization of Rome, when at the height of its strength and splendor, and when entirely oblivious to danger, was being steadily, though slowly, undermined; and was inevitably doomed to give place to a new order, born of a new and despised creed. It is well known that the patricians, the philosophers and even the plebs of the eternal city, held in contempt a religion that had a cross for its altar and an alleged malefactor for its hero. But notwithstanding this supercilious self-confidence, Christianity, weak, unattractive, and unostentatious, was destined to triumph and to give to history a new channel and a new course of development."[3]

How completely has it triumphed! How it has revolutionized the laws, the customs, the ideas, the very feelings of men until it has marvellously improved their condition. Well

---

[3] P. 60, 61.

may Lowell say: "There cannot be found a place on this planet ten miles square, where a decent man can live in decency, comfort and security, supporting and educating his children, unspoiled and unpolluted; a place where age is revered, infancy protected, manhood respected, womanhood honored, and life held in due regard—where the Gospel of Christ has not gone and cleared the way, laid the foundations and made decency and security possible."

CHRISTIANITY AND INTELLECTUALITY.

Now we sometimes hear it claimed, that a greater degree of intellectuality has been attained in the past than has yet been produced under the enlightening influence of revealed religion. What if it prove true? Christianity shall never bow down before it, for who does not know that the intellectuality of passed ages was hopelessly mixed with debauchery and every kind of wickedness. To-day the worldly exalt the intellectual, but Christianity would humble even them, because sin is universal, and they are not excluded from its power; because the educated and the gifted are truly said to have done more to bring dishonor upon civilization and to threaten society with ruin than the unendowed; because again it is true that "perverted education, misdirected shrewdness and calculating self-regard," can do more to trouble and degrade mankind than can possibly be equalled by the desperation of poverty and the evil design of illiteracy combined.

We unhesitatingly admit, however, that the world had learned much in the way of art and literature before the advent of the Light of the world, and that Greek culture and Roman jurisprudence have had a marked influence over even our present civilization. But when we hear men bemoaning the lost arts and saying, *e.g.*, that we never again shall see the equal of the pyramids of Egypt or the hanging gardens of Babylon, we can but say (albeit somewhat impatiently) that Christianity is not concerned with such things.

Christianity aims to build character, to teach men how to live righteously. It does not ignore the intellectual in man, nor has it any controversy with all true science. It encourages to the utmost, if it does not take the lead, in the effort to teach man "how to speak, how to write, how to think, how to build cathedrals, paint pictures, and compose sweet songs;" and the educational feature is a strong characteristic of all its foreign missions, but it especially teaches men how to curb their passions, how to restrain their violence, how to enjoy their freedom, how to promote the well being of one another. In a word, it would knit into one communion and fellowship the world of men, through the mystical Body of Christ. It would destroy enmities, dispel all variance, heal all differences and bind all classes and conditions of men into one loving and beloved brotherhood, under the Fatherhood of God, through Jesus Christ. It teaches that the only warfare to be maintained is that against the common enemy of mankind, sin; while it strives to lessen the ills and woes of man, to assuage pain and sorrow, to dispel darkness and misery. It would suppress all injustice and selfishness in man and enlarge his sympathies, provoke him to deeds of beneficence, and instill in him the principles of rectitude, that men may live soberly, righteously and godly in this present world."

THE KINGDOM OF CHRIST.

Again, with the author of *Ecce Homo*, we ask: What is the Kingdom of Christ?

"It is a world which, whatever its sins, its distance from ideal excellence, has recognized as the standard of its actions the law, which the Son of God spake on the Mount; a world where before His coming only a few wise and good men held somewhat of these precepts, and dreamed, like Plato, of an imaginary republic, but never in their wildest thoughts believed that society could be other than the selfish, and corrupt, and earthly thing they saw about them; yet every one of these lofty maxims has mastered the conscience of men, every one has been received as the acknowledged pattern of private, of social, of human goodness; when every good thus far attained has sprung from the unselfish spirit there enjoined, and even in the midst of unbelief, of superstition, of worldly policy, this spirit to-day labors not in vain; when every reform in the outward condition of mankind, every hope of liberty, and peace, and social justice is but the undespairing aim of men who believe that there is such a thing as a redeemed humanity; and this Christendom with its blessings, its hopes, its toils, its immortal aspirations, is the growth of the Word He spoke on the Mount, He wrought on the Cross. *Ecce Homo!* Behold the Man! Behold the religion of the Son of God and the Saviour of mankind."

ANTI-CHRISTIAN CULTS AND THEIR ADHERENTS.

Behold the religion that men would give up. From this, they turn aside to be comforted by the unreal in Spiritualism, to be mystified by the wonders of Theosophy, to be captivated by the deceptive cures of Christian Science.

What these anti-Christian cults, which are making inroads into the Household of Faith are, we shall attempt to show in succeeding chapters. We would now simply seek to know who they are that have recourse to them.

First; there are those who would gladly be rid of the sense of responsibility for the deeds done in the flesh. They may approve of what is right but they do not do it. They like neither to be compelled to do what is right in the sight of God nor to suffer the consequences of the evil that they have done. This is the law of God and man, but they would readily be attracted by any cult that claimed to destroy the reality of sin or that so expanded the idea of God as to destroy His Personality and make of Him an all-comprehensive and all-comprehending nonentity. It is useless, however. We must all appear before the judgment seat of Christ, that "every one may receive the things done in his body, according to that he has done, whether it be good or bad."

Next, there are those, poor souls, not well grounded in the faith, who know not what the Church and Bible teach, who have not experienced the comforts of religion and are ignorant of the purposes of the Almighty. When afflictions come upon them, or even adversity, they cannot realize that the Almighty may have meant it for some good end, as He does not willingly afflict or grieve the children of men. At first they are stunned, next they rebel, then they turn from the only help in time of need, to the vanities and deceptions of human ingenuity.

The last class are those who see not in the religion of Jesus something to be incorporated into and give true character to their daily life, something to carry them out of themselves into the world of loving sympathy and beneficence, whose indolence and selfishness are at the root of all their ills. These might interest themselves in the mysterious and uncanny or they would selfishly assent to any system or cult that would rid the world of all pain and suffering. Do they not know that the Master Himself "went not up to joy but first He suffered pain: He entered not into glory before He was crucified? So truly our way to eternal life is to suffer here with Christ."[4] It is the will of God. His eternal purpose cannot be changed. He sent His Son into the world that the world through Him might be saved. He sent His Son to be the Light of the world and marvellously has He dispelled the darkness. Let us then not be led astray and deceived by the false counsel and works that be of men, but let us open our hearts more and more to the truth as it is in Jesus, that we may be forever illuminated by the light of truth and life.

---

[4] Prayer Book Office for the Sick.

Spiritualism.

ITS CLAIMS, MANIFESTATIONS AND PHENOMENA.

THE problem of life and death is indeed a mystery. What is before us? How are we to triumph over the temptations that allure us, the difficulties that beset us and the obstacles that lie in our path, so as to accomplish the purpose for which we were sent into the world? But above all, what becomes of us? What are man's condition and circumstances after death?

A DEAD FAITH.

With a dead, worthless faith, many go through life, carelessly indifferent to these things, living in the narrow, selfish enjoyment of the hope of temporalities. Without the comforts and benefits of a holy Christian living, they are suddenly brought in pain and sorrow to confront the great problems of life. With no preparation, they ask with a cry, that pierces our hearts: "What is the purpose of life? What is the meaning of death? Where is my loved one? Why, if there is a God, was I not warned and prepared for this great trouble that is come upon me?" Painfully they are made to realize, at such a time, the truth of S. Paul's words: "Now we see through a glass darkly," enigmatically, as every phase of life is then an enigma to them. Hopelessly they admit that "now we know in part," and what they do not know of life, makes it full of mystery to them. The only solution is through faith in Jesus Christ, but they have not learned to walk by faith rather than by knowledge; their faith is dead, and so the door of peace, and comfort, and hope is closed to them. We cannot chide them, but we do pity them and pray that the Almighty "who does not willingly afflict or grieve the children of men," would sanctify this affliction to their good, and in spite of their faithlessness, selfishness and rebelliousness, might "so fetch them home" again to His flock that they might henceforth enjoy the "comfort of a reasonable, religious and holy hope." I say: "Fetch them home again," because they know that there is a much more perfect vision, a much more complete knowledge than that now vouchsafed them; but they are not willing to wait, till all shall be revealed. They want to know now and so they turn from the religion of Jesus Christ to attempt the impossible and seek through forbidden ways to peer into that which Almighty God has concealed behind an impenetrable veil.

SPIRITUALISM.

Their faithlessness, their despair, their eagerness for more light makes them easy, not to say willing, victims of that relic of those ancient heathen religions, whose priests trafficked upon the ignorance and superstition of the people, who lived in darkness and had not yet seen the Great Light. I refer, of course, to Spiritualism. It is not new. It has existed in some form or other almost from man's infancy. It is based upon the assumption that the spirits of the dead can and do communicate with the living, through the agency of peculiarly constituted persons called mediums, and that certain physical phenomena, which transcend all known natural laws, are produced by direct action of spirits or by spiritualistic power imparted to mediums, or others peculiarly susceptible to such influence. A partial truth lies at the root of this error, for the spirit of man does not die, but continues to exist after separation from the body; in addition to this, we are more influenced by spiritual powers, as we go through the earth-life, than we imagine.

Aside from these facts, we see in Spiritualism nothing but useless and profitless imposition, deceit and trickery, accompanied by most mercenary motives. Moreover, if these mediums are influenced by spiritualistic powers, they are the powers of darkness not of the light, for they are subject (if at all) to evil spirits and not to the spirits of departed saints.

MODERN SPIRITUALISM.

Spiritualism was revived in, or, we may say, Modern Spiritualism dates from 1848, through the Voss or Fox sisters of Hydesville, New York, who called attention to the various rappings that occurred when they were present, and who devised a code of communication whereby conversation could be carried on with the supposed intelligence alleged to produce these sounds. From this circumstance, quite an impetus was given to Spiritualism and large numbers of circles were established both in this country and in Europe. To what purpose are these circles or seances held! Manifestly to record the wonderful table tipping, raps, automatic writing with pencil or planchette or ouija board, writings in a folded slate without visible means, trance-speaking or letter-writing; the production of physical phenomena, such as lights, musical sounds, playing upon visible or invisible instruments, bringing flowers or other material objects into closed rooms, the materialization of hands or complete human figures, spirit photography, floating in the air without visible means of support, etc. Such manifestations and phenomena, it is claimed, prove the genuineness of spiritualistic communications; and such communications are alleged to be the attested proof of the survival of the departed who furnish instruction in moral and philosophical knowledge.

SPIRITUALISM OF NO BENEFIT SPIRITUALLY, MENTALLY, INTELLECTUALLY.

Now in the first place, we have reason to thank God that the reality of the life beyond the grave does not depend upon the flimsy prop of Spiritualism, but on the fact of the resurrection of Jesus Christ.

In the second place, what moral benefit could possibly follow from these alleged spiritualistic manifestations, the purpose of which is to attempt that which God in

His wise providence hath thought wise not to permit, or to make clear that which God will not now reveal? What comfort can the afflicted possibly derive from the materialization of a hand or arm or even of the whole body of a departed friend, which cannot be touched, but must be viewed in the dim, uncertain light in which evil revels? What solace can be derived from the silly twaddle said to be a message from the spirit-land? What lack of considerateness, not to say love, is manifest in the alleged spirits of our departed communicating with us through a third party, a stranger, and then only upon the assurance that like the Gypsy fortune-teller, we must cross the hand of the medium with silver? Unfortunately the days of superstition and humbuggery are not over, and it would seem that the people like to be deceived, even as Jeremiah said of old: "The prophets prophesy falsely and the priests bear rule by their means and my people love to have it so."[1]

---

[1] Jer. v. 31.

But surely, there can be no moral grandeur, no uplifting of the soul, no broadening of the mind, no advance in the way of righteousness, not even any real or lasting comfort in such things as these. In fact in no respect has Spiritualism enlightened, advanced or benefitted mankind.

In the third place, as to knowledge, moral or philosophical, Spiritualism affords none. It has done, it is doing, nothing for the intellectual improvement of mankind; it is not a benefit mentally or morally. Indeed its manifestations are not from the spirit-land and its phenomena are in no sense supernormal.

IT IS DECEPTION.

Its spirit rappings are declared to be physiological, as one of the Fox sisters is said to have admitted that the rapping by which they started the modern phase of Spiritualism was produced by a dislocation of their knee or other joints and suddenly snapping them back again.[2]

---

[2] Before her death she is said to have retracted this confession.

Slate-writing is simply a trick of legerdemain, spirit letter-writing is deceit, spirit photograph nothing but composite pictures, materialization undoubted trickery, while many mediums, having been worsted, have admitted that they practiced deceit.

INVESTIGATIONS.

Most intelligent commissions have investigated the claims of Spiritualism. The Leybert commission, from the University of Pennsylvania, after a thorough yet unprejudiced examination, declared that they could not discover a single novel fact and that they could employ men to do the same things done by mediums. The Italian commission, before whom the Neapolitan medium, Madame Palladino, held sittings, was rather unsatisfactory, some being convinced of the supernormal character of the phenomena, others being unable to offer any satisfactory explanation. This may seem to favor the claims of spiritualists who seek to convince by ocular demonstration, not by unassailable testimony; but the same claim can be made by prestidigitators. With them, we know it is trickery; or rather skill in deceiving their audiences, they admit it; yet we cannot explain how it is done. Moreover, the most expert of them stand ready to duplicate any phenomenon done by mediums, and that not by occult powers, but their own skill. We know too that the jugglers of India and Egypt are marvellous adepts, but we do not know that any supernormal powers are at their command. [3] The story has been published of the great prestidigitator, Kellar, seeing an Egyptian juggler perform a hanging in the open before a multitude, when the rope came down from above, as from the clouds, at his command. No success in the attempt to explain this feat was made by Kellar until he brought a mirror with him, and when it did not reflect the rope (showing that there was indeed no rope to be reflected) Kellar concluded the whole throng was hypnotized. The field of hypnotism, or mesmer-

---

[3] Narrated from memory.

ism, presents the widest opportunities for deception, for making things that are not, as though they did appear, for making people see things that are not. It affords ample opportunity for bewildering and deceiving people, but without the necessity of having recourse to spiritualistic communications at all. If there be anything in what is known as the odylic force—that mysterious power developed in connection with the brain as the nerve centre, and by which it was attempted to account for the phenomena of animal magnetism—it is only another link in the chain of evidence that demonstrates that these mysterious phenomena are distinctly physiological, and in no way dependent upon spiritualistic communication.

LIFE'S MYSTERIES AND SPIRITUALISM'S UNSUBSTANTIATED CLAIMS.

We need not to be assured of the truth of S. Paul's assertions, "now we see through a glass darkly . . . . now we know in part." Life is full of mysteries, and what little we see reflected as we are passing through, makes it one vast enigma. We are puzzled, perplexed. We know so little that it seems to make the problem of life the more difficult of solution.

We would know more, and Spiritualism comes forward with the claim that it can communicate with those beyond the veil, and through such means is enabled to clear our vision and give us that more perfect knowledge that we crave. It would substantiate its claims, not by unassailable testimony, but by ocular demonstration, by manifestations and phenomena. But these evidences have so often been detected as fraudulent, mediums have so repeatedly admitted trickery, commissions have so many times declared that there was nothing supernatural therein, prestidigitators so confidently declared their ability to reproduce any phenomena said to be done by spiritualistic power and have substantiated such claims, there are so many ways by which all these things may be shown to be physiological phenomena, that the conclusion is irresistible: Spiritualism does not and cannot substantiate its claims. Its manifestations and phenomena in no sense prove that they are due to spiritualistic communications or powers.

CHRIST THE SOLUTION.

We, however, are passing through this earth-life but once. Who then, amid all the trials, sorrows, perplexities and mysteries of life, can afford to place any confidence, can hope for any comfort, from that which is surrounded with so much fraud, deceit and unsubstantiated claims?

On the other hand, Luthardt, in *Fundamental Truths* says: "Man is a question; the word of Christ is its answer. Man is an enigma; the word of Christ is its solution. In an algebraical equation of three known quantities and one unknown, viz., X, the value of X being found, the correctness of the solution is proven by its perfect accordance with the other quantities. And the case here is exactly parallel. The word of Christ satisfies the equation of our nature; it is the solution of the X, of the unknown quantity within us."

Let us not, then, ask for the impossible or try to circumvent God and peer into the unknown, but let us walk by faith through life; with Christ as our guide, let us abide in the truth as it is in Him. Then may we look confidently forward to the time when we shall see face to face "and know as we are known."

Spiritualism. 11.

SUBJECTION TO SPIRITS.

IN considering the manifestations and phenomena whereby it is attempted to show the power of Spiritualism, we found the claims of spiritual communication not proven and the manifestation and phenomena so surrounded with trickery, deceit and fraud, as to be unworthy of any consideration whatever. Continuing the subject of Spiritualism, we would say of those honest, earnest and learned men who accept the claims of spiritualistic communications in good faith, that the weight of evidence is against them and that men, learned men, may be earnest, sincere, positive, and yet be mistaken.

SPIRITUAL EXISTENCE.

We believe in spiritual existence most certainly. We believe that we still shall live, though the body crumble in the dust. S. Paul, speaking by inspiration, says: "Put on the whole armor of God that ye may be able to stand against the wiles of the devil. For we wrestle, not against flesh and blood, but against the principalities, against the powers, against the world rulers of this darkness, against the spiritual hosts of wickedness in the heavenly places." Thus forcibly is declared a super-terrestrial existence, that the air is infested with these immaterial beings, whose purpose is to tempt, to deceive, to lead astray.

If these be the fallen angels, then there is the multitude of the heavenly host, who left not their first estate. And no one will dispute the assertion that in the doctrine of angels, yea in the very being of God, the Bible teaches spiritual existences.

MAN'S SPIRIT.

Man is made in the image of his God. That image must be spiritual, as God is Spirit, and it is the spiritual in man that does not die.[1]

Where, then, does man's spirit go at death? It is not left to roam in the earth or to drift through the air. Christ said to the penitent thief upon the Cross: "To-day shalt thou be with Me in Paradise," the beautiful Garden of Eden, transferred from earth, the abode of the blessed saints in light.

Moreover, S. Peter declared that during those three days when our blessed Lord's spirit was separated in death from His human body, He went and preached unto the spirits in prison.[2] In our Lord's parable of the rich man and Lazarus, we find the rich man, after death, to be in a place of torments, from which there was no escape and which was separated from the place where Lazarus and Abraham were (Paradise) by "a great gulf."[3] These passages would indicate that the spirits of the departed are confined in a region, beyond the earth, yet short of heaven, which

---

[1] See Heb. xi. 39, 40; Matt. xxii. 30.
[2] I. S. Pet. iii. 19.   [3] S. Luke xvi. 23.

the Church defines (none too definitely, because she knows only in part) as the "place of departed spirits."

THE INTERMEDIATE STATE.

We next inquire: "What has ever been learned concerning this Intermediate State from those who have appeared from the dead? *Absolutely nothing.* Moses and Elijah, who appeared on the Mount of the Transfiguration and were seen of Peter, James and John, talked only with the Lord.

We turn to the son of the widow of Zarephath, to the son of the widow of Nain, to Lazarus, the brother of Martha and Mary, whose body lay four days in the grave, and we find their lips sealed. There were those who came forth from the grave at the resurrection, but they left not a word for living humanity.

Calling to mind S. Paul's being caught up into the "third heaven" and "hearing unspeakable words" which he declared "it was not lawful for a man to utter,"[4] shall we not be

---
[4] II. Cor., xii. 2-4.

justified in concluding that the uniform silence of those who have tasted of death, is because it is "not lawful" for men to speak on such matters; it is forbidden of God?

Moreover, in our Lord's parable, we remember Dives pleaded with Abraham to send Lazarus to his five brothers, who were still living, "that he may testify unto them lest they also come into this place of torment." To his plea: "If one went unto them from the dead, they will repent," Abraham replies: "If they hear not Moses and the prophets, neither will they be persuaded, though one rose from the dead."

COMMUNICATING WITH THE DEAD.

As the Lord gave the Jews Moses and the prophets, so He hath given us the Church and the Bible, to lead us into the way of truth and life. These are more persuasive than one returning from the dead; and the inference is plain, that no communication shall be sent from the dead to help those who will not be satisfied with the Gospel of Jesus Christ. For in that Gospel we behold the merciful

God's message to fallen men that alone can be effectual in turning them from their sins.

Moreover, it is impossible to find in the Holy Scriptures *any sanction* for the *consultation of the dead*. Moses and Elijah on the Mount of the Transfiguration represented the saints of the Lord, both being clothed in glorified bodies like His own; but when Peter would make them tabernacles, indicating that he would have them remain and abide on earth again, behold the vision was swept from his sight by a cloud, out of which was heard the Voice: "This is My Beloved Son; hear ye *Him;*" thus plainly teaching that they should seek Him alone.

Again, with the possible exception of Samuel (and we firmly believe that Saul was deceived, possibly hypnotized, when he thought he "perceived Samuel appearing to him through the machinations of the witch of Endor"[5])—with this possible exception, there is not in Scripture the slightest intimation of even the possibility of any communica-

---

[5] I. Sam., xxviii.

tion between the departed in the Lord and those who still remain on earth.

More than this, the Bible nowhere intimates that the departed can even see what may be taking place on the earth. "In one instance" says Pember, "it seems to be assumed that they *cannot*. For the Good Shepherd, after finding the lost sheep, calls His friends and neighbors and bids them rejoice with Him. Now His neighbors are probably the angels, for they dwell where He is, and it is not unlikely that the spirits in paradise are His friends. 'Henceforth,' He said to His disciples, 'I call you not servants: for the servant knoweth not what his lord doeth: but I have called you friends; for all things that I have heard of My Father, I have made known unto you.'[6] It would seem, then, that whenever any poor wanderer is brought back to the fold, the Lord calls the spirits of his relatives and friends who have already entered into rest, tells them that the lost is found, and rejoices with them in the

---

[6] S. John xv. 15.

knowledge that His beloved and theirs is reconciled to the Father, and will soon join their happy and never ending fellowship. But if it be necessary for Christ to announce this good news to the blessed spirits, it is clear that they *cannot* be watching their friends who are still in the flesh."[7]

ANGELS.

Scripture speaks repeatedly, however, of the ministry of angels, but we are to bear in mind that they communicate with man not of their own volition, or because influenced by man, but as the express messengers of God, sent of Him for some specific purpose, sent to reveal God's eternal truth. But angels are *not disembodied spirits*, neither are they the glorified forms of the departed of this world. They are a *distinct creation*, nor can we be like unto them until after the resurrection.[8]

EVIL SPIRITS AND DEMONS.

But the Scriptures do also speak in no uncertain measures of evil spirits which war

---

[7] *Earth's Earliest Ages*, 344.   [8] S. Luke xx. 35, 36.

against the soul and seek to lead men to destruction, and S. Paul urges us to put on the whole armor of God, because we have to wrestle against "the spiritual hosts of wickedness in the heavenly places,"[9] who are undoubtedly emissaries of "the prince of the power of the air, the spirit that now worketh in the children of disobedience."[10]

If, therefore, as S. Paul says: "The working of Satan is with all power and signs and lying wonders,"[11] and the air swarms with rebellious spirits, though they be forbidden to communicate with man, or to influence him to evil, we need not be surprised at the disobedience, occasional manifestation and open interference in the affairs of men, of these rebellious spirits.

I.—SCRIPTURAL REFERENCE TO COLLUSION BETWEEN EVIL SPIRITS AND MEN.—O. T.

In the Scriptures we find repeated allusions to the dealings between men and evil spirits, and of the latter taking pos-

---

[9] Eph. vi. 12 (R.V.). [10] Eph. ii. 2.
[11] II. Thess. ii. 9 (R.V.).

session of the former. In the enumeration of those who thus have fellowship with demons, and thereby claim supernormal powers, Pember enumerates "the sacred scribes;"[12] said to be identical with the medium writers of to-day; "the wise men;"[13] wizards, who claimed greater than human power through intercourse with supernatural beings; the diviners by omens or spirit communications; the mesmerist, obtaining oracles through his subject; the augurs, divining by flight of birds, etc.; those using incantations or magical formulas; the spell binders, who used charms or amulets; the consulters of demons; the knowing ones (*i.e.*, through associating with spirits); the necromancers or seekers of the dead; the whisperers or mutterers; the star-gazers; the deliverers of monthly predictions from observations; the sorcerers and astrologers, mentioned by Daniel.

II.—N. T. REFERENCE.

In the New Testament, mention is made of the magi, priests who interpreted dreams and

---
[12] Gen. xli. 8.   [13] Ex. vii. 11.

omens, who were soothsayers, who seemed to be acquainted with the practices of modern spiritualism; the pharmacists, those who use drugs, whether for poisoning or as a magic potion, who were sorcerers; and those who practiced curious magical arts and trafficked in amulets. "It will be observed," says Pember, "that demoniacal arts fall readily into three classes. The first comprises all kinds of divination by omens, tokens and forbidden sciences; the second, the use of spells and incantations as a means of accomplishing what is desired; and the third, every method of direct and intelligent communication and coöperation with demons."[14]

I.—SCRIPTURAL CONDEMNATION OF COMMUNICATION WITH EVIL SPIRITS.—O. T.

Pember believes in the willing communication of men with evil spirits or demons, and the Bible would seem to admit and condemn the practice. "Thou shalt not suffer a

---

[14] See Pember's *Earth's Earliest Ages*, pp. 256-265.

witch to live,"[15] says the Law. And, again, "A man or a woman that hath a familiar spirit, or that is a wizard, shall surely be put to death; they shall stone them with stones; their blood be upon them."[16]

Again, the Lord declared of the Levites that they should not learn to do after the abomination of the nations in the land of promise: "There shall not be found among you any one that maketh his son or his daughter to pass through fire, or that useth divination or an observer of times, or an enchanter, or a witch, or a charmer, or a consulter with familiar spirits, or a wizard, or a necromancer."[17]

The frequent condemnation in the Law of the practices of all kinds of sorcery was necessary in order to destroy the influence of the Egyptian art among the chosen people, and to prepare them against similar arts in the land of promise.

Saul, probably at the instigation of Samuel, set about to exterminate these evil-doers

---

[15] Ex. xxii. 18.   [16] Lev. xx. 27.   [17] Deut. xviii. 10, 11.

so vigorously, that the few that survived practised only in secret. And if, in his distress at his latter end, Saul himself consulted the witch of Endor, we are told the crime sealed his doom.[18]

II.—CONDEMNATION IN N. T.

If in the Old Testament witches, necromancers, dealers with familiar spirits and sorcerers of any and all kinds are commanded to be destroyed, so in the New Testament we read that "the fearful and unbelieving and the abominable .... and sorcerers and idolators and all liars are to have their part in the lake that burneth with fire and brimstone, which is the second death."

IDOLATRY AND DEMONOLOGY.

1. This entire system of abominations was found of old to be associated with idolatry. Now the Bible does assuredly seem to recognize spiritual existences behind the idols of heathenism and declares that these existences are demons. It does not dispute therefore the *fact of their being* but the truth of their pre-

---

[18] I. Chron. x. 13.

tensions. Thus the Lord is said to have punished the gods of the Egyptians when he slew the first born of man and beast.[19] And when Jehovah is declared to be the "God of gods and Lord of lords,"[20] to be highly exalted above all gods, to be feared above all gods, it must be that these gods, with whom He is contrasted, are real existences. In Deut. xxxii. 17 it is said, "They sacrificed unto demons, not to God; to gods whom they knew not;" and Ps. xcvi. 5, according to the Septuagint, reads: "For all the gods of the nations are *demons* but the Lord made the heavens."

2. In the New Testament S. Paul says: "For though there be beings called gods, whether in heaven or upon earth—as there actually are gods many and lords many—yet to us there is One God the Father—and One Lord Jesus Christ."[21]

Again, it is S. Paul that says: "The things which the Gentiles sacrifice, they sacrifice to demons, and not to God; and I do not wish

---
[19] Ex. xii. 12; Num. xxxiii. 4.
[20] Deut. x. 17.   [21] I. Cor. viii. 4-6.

you to have communion with demons. Ye cannot drink the cup of the Lord and the cup of demons."[22]

As Pember says: "An idol, the creation of man's fancy, is nothing; but it is not possible that men could be moved to worship nothing; there is a real power behind them. The heathen think they are sacrificing to Deity; but their offerings ascend to demons, and by their sacrificial feasts, they establish a fellowship with unclean spirits, similar to that which exists between Christ and His Church. It is plain therefore that the *evil* spirits *which haunt the* air *are* the beings whom the heathen worship, the inspirers of oracles and sooth-sayers, the originators of all idolatry, the powers that are ever striving by divers means to subjugate the human race to their sway."[23]

SPIRITUALISM A PART OF THE SYSTEM OF DEMONOLOGY.

As we read the Scriptures understandingly then, we readily infer that from ancient time

---

[22] I. Cor. x. 19-21.   [23] *Earth's Earliest Ages*, 240.

aerial forms, visions, oracles, sooth-saying, spirit writing, voices of the unseen, magnetic healing, in fact, spirit communications, auguries, omens, tokens, lucky and unlucky days and numbers, potions, amulets, charms, fetiches, relics, are part of the countless prescriptions of demoniacal systems. But modern Spiritualism revels in spirit communications, spirit writings, visions, oracles and such like. Therefore modern Spiritualism too is part of this demoniacal system, part of the plan of Satan, to bring men under the influence of demons and evil spirits.

MIND READING.

But it is asked: How do you explain the wonderful things revealed by mediums concerning past and future? Dean Hart, of Denver, writes that when an undergraduate, spending his vacation in his father's parish in a Yorkshire dale, there came there a conjurer, Signor Barnado, with a clairvoyant who would describe articles given the conjurer by the audience or repeat sentences silently recited. A friend of the Dean's was at the time off at his trouting grounds. Knowing well the room in which he sat, the Dean wrote him to ask him to be examining his fly book at 9 o'clock P.M. At that hour the Dean stood up in the audience and said to the conjurer: "I have a friend thirty miles from here. I want to know what he is doing and where he is": declaring that he knew what his friend was about. Continuing in his own words: "He put the question to the blindfolded girl, and she began to describe my friend to the life, fresh face, his blue spotted necktie, his gold spectacles, the mahogany furniture, the green figured cloth on the table, the fluted silver candlesticks; he was reading a book. 'What is it about?' asked Barnado. 'I do not know' said the girl. 'Turn to the title page and read it.' 'There is no title page.' Then suddenly after a short pause, she said, 'It's about fly-fishing.' Now, I said, what is the name of the village? Barnado asked me if I would tell him, and he would stand near me, and away from the platform, but I replied that I preferred not to do so. He then asked the girl if she could tell, and after a moment or two, she rightly replied: 'Pateley Bridge.' As this very interesting episode was in progress, I found she was reading my mind. As I arranged the furniture in the room, so did she; as I pictured the fluted silver candlesticks, so exactly she described them; and if I had put on the end of my tongue that my friend was fishing at Timbuctoo, she would have said so."[24]

Thus was the power of the medium explained without the aid of spirits. And we firmly believe that all their wonderful power of healing and revealing can be explained by means of the subjective mind, the doubled consciousness and hypnotic suggestion.

COMMUNICATIONS FROM EVIL SPIRITS ADMITTEDLY FALLIBLE AND UNRELIABLE.

If there can be anything supernormal in Spiritualism, however, it is due *not* to communication with the *spirits of our blessed dead*

---

[24] "A Way That Seemeth Right." Hart. pp. 53-54.

but to *evil spirits*, to *demons* who are evidently lying in wait to deceive. Thus, Croesus, the king of Lydia, is said to have consulted the Delphic oracle before giving battle to the king of Persia. The Pythoness declared: "Croesus, if he cross the Halys, will destroy a great empire." Too late he learned that the empire to be destroyed was his own.

Ah, whoever consults with evil that does not have to pay dearly for it! For these utterances of demons are always uncertain, deceitful and meant so to be. So true is this, that a canon of Spiritualism reads: "That communications from the spirit world, whether by mental impression, inspiration, or any other mode of transmission, are *not necessarily infallible truth;* but, on the contrary, partake unavoidably of the imperfections of the minds from which they emanate, and of the channels through which they come, and are, moreover, liable to misrepresentation by those to whom they are addressed."[25]

---

[25] See *Earth's Earliest Ages* 339.

If this is not a sufficient admission of the unreliability of such alleged communications, then T. L. Harris, in the *Spiritualist*, for June 25th, 1875, writes: " There is no dependence to be placed on the mere verbal statements of spirits as to their real belief. One class deceives purposely; they are simply flowing into your general thought, and coinciding with devout convictions, for the purpose of obtaining a supreme and ruinous dominion over your mind and body. Another class are simply parasites, negatives, drawn into the personal sphere of the medium, and seeking to sun themselves in its light and heat by absorbing the vital forces, on which they feed, and by. means of which they, for a time, revive their faded intelligence and apathetic sense. To the Mohammedan, they confirm the Koran; to the Pantheist, they deify nature; to the believer in the Divine Humanity they glorify the Word." If these demons do reveal things through mediums how utterly unreliable and useless such revelation is.

PURPOSE OF DEMONS TO DECEIVE.

In the case of demoniacal possession, of which mention is made repeatedly in the New Testament, the demon at times assumes complete control over the subject in whom it dwells. When cast out, as in the case of the Philippian damsel, who had a spirit of divination (*lit.*, Pythonian spirit), which S. Paul cast out,[26] the subject has no longer this alleged supernormal power.

If, therefore, these demons take possession of human subjects in order to interfere with the affairs of men, if their purpose is to deceive, if they are so uncertain that no dependence can be placed in them, if they can only give opinions and are compelled to confess that they know no more than we do, why should any mortal be so wickedly foolish as to waste time, money and faith consulting them?

If, in the whole Bible, there is not a single instance of these spirits of the air influencing men for good, in the words of Isaiah why

---
[26] Acts xvi. 16-20.

should we inquire of them that have familiar spirits and of wizards that chirp and mutter: should not a people inquire of their God? For the living should they inquire of the dead?[27]

GOD'S CONDEMNATION OF THE PRACTICE OF CONSULTING DEMONS.

Moreover, has not God said in the terrible words of the Law: "The soul that turneth after such as have familiar spirits, and after wizards, to go a whoring after them, I will even set My Face against that soul, and will cut him off from among his people?" Thus would God punish those who consult demons.

SPIRITUALISM ANTI-CHRISTIAN.

Now the great abomination of this Spiritualism, ancient and modern, is that it is founded in direct defiance of the laws of God, and is based upon an idolatrous substitution of evil spirits (demons) for the Living God.

But we have called it Anti-Christian, and S. John declares: "This is Anti-Christ, who denieth the Father and the Son." We have

---

[27] Is. viii. 19.

already seen how it adapts itself to Mohammedan, Pantheist, or Christian, as the case may be. As for the Christ, it ignores Him as the Saviour of mankind. It speaks of the Son of God as a divine efflux, of the Father and the Son as one Person, of Christ as a powerful medium and as a teacher to be classed with Buddha, Confucius, Zoroaster. It blasphemously alleges of the Holy Spirit, that He is the female element in the Godhead or that He is the Holy Breath. It would put communicating spirits (demons) in the place of God the Holy Spirit.

Notwithstanding the Gospel declares that "now is the accepted time," and that the Lord warns us that the destiny of man is fixed in the intermediate state—in the joys of Paradise or in the throes of the place of torment—Spiritualism teaches that man may repair in that state the errors of a mis-spent pilgrimage on earth, and that he passes through seven spheres.[28]

It teaches that "all crime is unpardonable

---

[28] *Earth's Earliest Ages*, 364.

and could only be wiped out by *personal and not by vicarious atonement*, as falsely taught"[29] in Holy Scripture.

Thus it is seen that Spiritualism, though outwardly tolerant, is really opposed to Christianity. It would destroy belief in God and the Saviour. It would substitute for revealed religion a cult that abounds in deceit, trickery and fraud, and that is unscathingly condemned and forbidden in the Bible. It claims ability to reveal that which God has not made known, by a power given through communication with the spirits of the departed. It has, and can have, no communication with the spirits of those who are, according to the Bible, imprisoned in the *place* of *departed spirits*. If it has any supernormal powers at all, it is due to demons who take possession of mediums, evil spirits, the spiritual hosts of wickedness in heavenly places, against whom we wrestle, the emissaries of the Prince of the powers of the air, and the Prince of this world, against whose

---

[29] *Ghost Land*, p. 43.

wiles we need to put on the whole armor of God, that we may be able to stand.

While we may not be able to define the powers of these evil spirits, yet we know, from the admission of spiritualists, that their communications are "*not* infallible truth," but partake of "imperfections," and that these spirits "deceive purposely"; yea, their purpose is primarily to deceive, to lead away from the truth, in order to strengthen the power and kingdom of Satan. And shall we willingly be deceived?

Ah, trust not to lying lips and deceitful tongues. There is much that we would like to know about this world with its sorrow, toil and pain, but a merciful God has willed it otherwise. It is not necessary, it is not best for us, therefore we will not forsake God and the Saviour, to be imposed upon by those who claim power to peer beyond the impenetrable veil and reveal what God wills not to reveal. Instead we will accept God's plan of salvation and redemption, and trusting upon a merciful Father, leaning on a loving Saviour, comforted by the sanctifying Spirit, we will, by the grace given us, strive to fulfil our destiny in life, do good in our generation and look confidently forward to a reunion with our dear departed, and to the time when we shall see face to face and know as we are known.

Theosophy. I.

ITS ORIGIN AND PURPOSE.

A FEW years ago heralds went forth throughout the land to proclaim, with sound of trumpets, a World's Parliament of Religions. It was to be held in connection with, an adjunct of, a sort of side light to, the World's Fair. It was seized upon by the promoters of the latter, just as anything else would have been, which they thought might be of financial benefit to them in their great undertaking. The real object, however, was not to advance the cause of that Divine organization, the Church Universal, which has done so much for the enlightenment and happiness of all mankind, which has shown itself to be the leaven which can and is, gradually yet surely, leavening the whole world, but in the hope that it might pave the way for a sort of composite religion of *man's* concoction and an universal brotherhood.

Strange; but it is not an original idea, for one of the alleged purposes of the Theosophical Society is to form the nucleus of an Universal Brotherhood.

THEOSOPHY DEFINED.

Theosophy, as its name implies, is contrary to the generally accepted views of S. Paul concerning the wisdom and knowledge of God, that His judgments are unsearchable and His ways past finding out.[1] Theosophy is one of those wisdom religions which claim to have "special (if not complete) insight into the Divine nature and its constitutive moments and processes." . . . . "The Science of the Wisdom of God." "It starts with an explication of the Divine essence and endeavors to deduce the phenom-

---

[1] Rom. xi. 33.

enal universe from the play of forces within the Divine nature itself."[2] "It sees no insolvable mystery anywhere, throws the words chance and coincidence out of its vocabulary, and affirms the omnipresence and omnipotence of law and perfect justice. It postulates an Eternal Principle, unknowable except in its manifestations, which is in and is all things and which, periodically and eternally, manifests itself and recedes from manifestation—evolution and involution. It affirms a spiritual condition after death and numberless flesh and blood lives on this and other planets. In its practical working, it is a most vicious fatalism. It destroys the freedom of the will. It leads man through the world (or worlds) according to inexorable law. It speaks of a justice that knows no mercy under any circumstances. Its doctrines are based upon the *ipse dixit* of an adept, a Mahatma, and there is no appeal from their "say so." It must be accepted absolutely.

---

[2] *En. Britannica.*

ITS CLAIMS AND ASSUMPTIONS.

The evolution of man is not, it claims, carried out on this planet alone, but is the result of many worlds and different conditions of spiritual and material development; and the earth is one link in the chain of many worlds. "All individual spiritual entities must pass through the successive worlds of the system." This is the evolution of man.

Theosophy is claimed to be a religion, a science and a philosophy: "A religion, because it aims to know, to become and therefore to worship, truth; a science, because it examines by strict analysis all processes in nature in order to discover that which is; a philosophy, because by logical synthesis from the facts of nature discovered by science, it discloses the laws that underlie phenomena and govern the universe."

Its tendency, however, is not to make the truth clearer, but to further mystify; it claims ability to explain all things, yet it does not do so, but asserts that man is not in a condition to understand; it assumes too many theories as facts ever to substantiate its claims. It assumes the theory of evolution; it assumes the doctrine of re-incarnations; it assumes that there are such beings as Mahatmas; that they can explain all mysteries, and that they can and do communicate with man. These fundamental principles of Theosophy are not, and cannot be, proven.

ORIGIN.

Moreover, Theosophy, this very old cult, is distinctly and avowedly pagan in its origin, and paganism is an emanation from the powers of the air, whose aim is the propagation of evil among men; and whose gods, though false, are real, as implied in the Bible, and are to be identified with the evil spirits which interfere with the affairs of men, so as to perplex, deceive and lead astray. Theosophy, then, might well be called an emanation or, considering its claims, a revelation of evil spirits.

Now, as in the days of Gnosticism, we know there was an attempt to bolster up the decaying heathen philosophy and religion by amalgamating with Christianity. So in these latter days, we find another attempt at amalgamation in the hope that Theosophy may be the leaven that will so permeate as to completely change the blessed religion of Jesus Christ.

"We are told," according to Pember in his admirable work on this subject, "that Occultism is the wisdom of primal ages, a revival of the only true philosophy, held by all the great teachers of the world and communicated to the Initiates of the Mysteries. And we are admonished that Christianity, although it did contrive to displace the old religions in the West, has proved a failure; and that we must, therefore, return to that which is better, and confess to the superiority of ancient sages."[3]

THE BROTHERHOOD.

By means of certain heathen symbols which Christianity has purified and pre-

---

[3] *Theosophy*, p. 36.

served, it is claimed that Occultism has been handed down from the times of the Mysteries to the present. "The only Brotherhood now mentioned in the outer world," says Pember, "is one which extends its branches throughout the East and of which the headquarters are reported to be in Thibet."[4] Through the advance of modern science and the development of evolutionary philosophy, which fitted men for further instruction, these Brothers determined to communicate with the world and influence its science and religion. They, however, were too "etherealized" to associate with "coarse human nature," therefore they must work through "intermediaries."

THE AMERICAN MISSION.

The first of these "intermediaries," we believe, was Madame Blavatski, grand-daughter of Princess Dolgorouki. Born in Northern Russia, in 1831, she married at seventeen, Gen. Blavatski, who was 43 years her senior.

---

[4] See *Earth's Earliest Ages* p. 400.

She left him after three months.[5] She is said to have spent thirty years in the study of occult pursuits and travel, and is reputed to have practiced Spiritualism. In 1857, she was undoubtedly in Thibet. The following year she was thrown from her horse and sustained a fracture of the spine, and her physical condition was such that we are not surprised that she was susceptible to hallucinations and queer notions. Then she spent seven years under the immediate direction of the Brothers; she was initiated, then instructed for her mission and finally sent out into the world to influence its religion and philosophy with the doctrines of Occultism. She seems to have come to America to begin her mission, and in 1875 formed the Theosophical Society.

ITS OBJECTS AND THEIR ATTAINMENTS.

The objects of the society are said to be threefold:

1. "To form the nucleus of a Universal Brotherhood without any distinction what-

---

[5] See *Theosophy*, p. 17.

ever," yet in undoubted opposition to the Brotherhood of man under the Fatherhood of God through Christ Jesus.

2. "To study ancient literature, religion and science"—evidently with the idea of destroying the claims of Christianity as the only true religion.

3. "To explore the hidden mysteries of Nature and the latent powers of man," with the idea of destroying belief in a personal God and Father of us all.

4. A fourth object, not as yet boldly affirmed, is the destruction of Christianity, declaring it, as we have seen, to be a failure, so that we should "return to that which is better and confess to the superiority of ancient sages."

If we ask, how are these objects being attained, we are referred to the work: *Hints on Esoteric Theosophy*,[6] in which we learn that in 1880 the Bombay branch sent a mixed delegation of Hindus and Parsees to assist in founding a Buddhist branch in Ceylon, and in

---

[6] See *Earth's Earliest Ages*, p. 403.

1881 the Buddhists reciprocated by sending delegates to Tinnevelly to assist in organizing Hindu branches, and that they, with Col. Olcott, the first American[7] captivated by Madame Blavatski, were "received with raptured welcome inside a most sacred Hindu Temple." This same work sends out the statement that in 1883 they had seventy branches in India "and many thousands of Mohammedans, Buddhists, Parsees, Christians, officials and non-officials, governors and governed, have been brought together by its instrumentality." Apparently they are satisfied with its levelling powers. Theosophy does not condemn any of these religions but would explain them. It would draw all men of whatever religions together on the same level, and so has its Buddhist branches, Hindu branches, Parsee branches. They are not asked to change their religions but simply to accept the theosophic explanation of them.

---

[7] In 1875 Col. Olcott went to Vermont, as representative of a New York paper, to investigate the spiritualistic manifestations of the Eddy Brothers. There he met Mme. Blavatski, and soon became a willing disciple.

Nominally Buddhists, Hindus, Parsees still, they are really Theosophists only. Thus they allow us to believe that one can be a Theosophist and a Christian at the same time, a manifest impossibility. See how it is working. It sets forth a universal brotherhood, a popular idea that attracts attention. It advises a study of the ancient world religions, to keep its adherents interested, with the possible idea of investigating for oneself and increasing one's knowledge; a worthy motive. It takes the symbols and doctrines so long cherished in the Western world and attempts to bring out an esoteric theosophic truth underlying the Christian error. Then, as published in *Isis Unveiled*,[8] it furnishes authenticated accounts of all crimes and misdemeanors, schisms and heresies, controversies and litigations, doctrinal differences and Biblical criticisms and revisions, with which the press in Christian lands teem, and sends them to "Palestine, India, Ceylon, Cashmere, Tartary, Thibet,

---

[8] *Isis Unveiled*, Vol. I., pp. 41-42.

China and Japan, in all of which countries it has influential correspondents." Its objects with us then, may all be reduced to one—the overthrow of Christianity and the supplanting of all other religions with the idea of establishing Theosophy or Occultism as the one religion of the world. This shall be brought about when the twelfth Messiah shall come and, harmonizing the perverted teachings of his predecessors, shall establish "an universal religion which shall recognize the Messiahs of all nations."

THEOSOPHY VS. CHRISTIANITY.

Behold, then the purpose of putting all religions, including Christianity, on a level, namely, that out of them as superior, yea, supreme, may be evolved an universal religion, and that, Theosophy.

With all our worldliness and insincerity, are we ready to give up the religion of Jesus Christ for any Eastern mysticism? Are we ready to put the religion of Jesus Christ on a level with those ancient religions which with all their claims, with all their age, have done and can do so little for the advancement of mankind? Are we ready to acknowledge the superiority of ancient sages, over the best thought of the Western world to-day? Are we ready to give up ourselves into the power of a system that claims ability to explain all things, yet cannot? Are we ready to return to heathen darkness and civilization? The one way to do so, is to give up the blessed religion of Jesus Christ. If you are not ready for these things, then "beloved . . . beware lest ye also being led away with the error of the wicked, fall away from your own steadfastness."

Theosophy II.

ITS LEADING DOCTRINES AND FALSE POSITION.

IN considering the origin and purpose of Theosophy, we found that it is of pagan conception, an attempt through the "superiority of ancient sages" to build up the old world religions, drag Christianity down to a level with them, and so harmonize them all, that out of them would spring an universal religion, which, necessarily would be Theosophy. It does not attack, directly, Christianity or any other of the world's religions but it would explain the doctrines and symbols that we hold so dear according to theosophical truth, which of course would eliminate every Christian belief, hope and purpose therefrom. We turn now to its doctrines.

DOCTRINES—A PERSONAL GOD.

First, as to our God and Father. We are told that the "'Father in heaven' is a well known esoteric phrase for the Higher Self, and to pray 'Our Father, who art in heaven' is, in the initiate's mouth, an attempt to 'meditate on and aspire to the Higher Self.'"

Theosophy does not, cannot, admit a personal God. It is based upon evolution and is pantheistic, as proclaimed by Mrs. Besant. To admit the Being of a personal God and Creator, the Supreme Ruler of the Universe, to whom all creatures do bow and obey, would be to destroy the claims of adepts, the authority of Mahatmas, and undermine the foundations upon which Theosophy stands; but to say: "God is all and all is God," while not a dangerous admission, is a convenient way of robbing the Deity of all authority, without denying Him actual existence, but the theosophist in denying a personal Deity must deny in reality the religion of Jesus Christ, the revelation of a personal God and Father.

The interplanetary ether, called in Occultism, arteal fluid, is declared to be the first manifestation of "Substance," that which sub-stands all phenomena; and its ultimate expression is what we call matter."[1] Spirit and matter are but different states of the *one* substance. The substance of soul and all things and the substance of Deity are the same. The life of this Substance is called God, who, being the Living Substance, is both Life and Substance, *i.e.*, two in one. What is called (theologically) the Son and the Word, which proceeds from these two, is "the expression of both and is potentially the Universe;" but the term, "Son of God," is a "title assumed by all Initiates, that implies the assimilation of the Ego and the Higher Self, as does the expression: 'I and My Father are One,'"[2] while the Holy Spirit

---

[1] See *The Perfect Way*, pp. 17, 18.
[2] See Preface to *Theosophy*.

is looked upon as the female element in the Deity.

CHRIST.

Christ is declared to be a title given to all triumphant initiates who have passed the symbolical crucifixion and have become the anointed masters of all nature.[3] Our blessed Lord then is declared to be simply an Initiate, not *the* Christ but *a* Christ or an adept who has passed through many transmigrations and has turned His life to best account by development of the higher faculties and qualities of man,[4] and He is associated with Osiris, Mithras, Crishna Dionysus and Buddha. Kenealy's *Commentary on the Apocalypse* mentions eleven Messiahs: Adam, Enoch, Fohi, Brigu, Zoroaster, Thoth, Moses, Lao-Tseu, Jesus, Mohammed and Chenzig-Khan. While these "Messengers" only affected particular nations for the most part, and their doctrines, through the corruption and ignorance of men, seemed contra-

---

[3] See Article in *Lucifer*, October, 1891.
[4] See *The Perfect Way*, p. 226.

dictory, yet a twelfth Messenger is to appear, who is to harmonize the perverted teachings of his predecessors and establish "a universal religion which shall recognize the messiahs of all 'nations.'"

THE TRINITY.

The doctrine of the Trinity is after this manner: "The Divine Substance is, in its original condition homogeneous. Every monad of it, therefore, possesses the potentialities of the whole. Of such a monad, in its original condition, every individual soul consists. And of the same Substance, projected into lower conditions, the material universe consists. It undergoes, however, no radical change of nature through such projection; but its manifestation—on whatever plane occurring—is always as a Trinity in Unity; since that whereby Substance becomes manifest is the evolution of its Trinity. Thus—to reckon from without inwards, and below upwards—on the plane physical, it is Force, universal Ether, and their offspring the Material

World. On the plane intellectual, it is Life, Substance, and Phenomenon. On the plane spiritual—its original point of radiation—it is Will, Wisdom and the Word. And on all planes whatever, it is, in some mode, Father, Mother, Child."[5] Thus with daring blasphemy would Theosophy "explain" to its own satisfaction the Christian doctrines concerning God, the Father Almighty, Maker of Heaven and earth and of all things visible and invisible, Jesus Christ His Only Son our Lord, and the Holy Spirit, the Lord and Giver of Life, three Divine Persons yet only one God.

MAN.

Turning to man, we find according to this revival of the ancient religions, which history comments on as one of the epidemics which break forth during the last quarter of a century—according to Theosophy, man is not a creation of God but the result of development in the process of evolution.

---

[5] *The Perfect Way*, pp. 17, 18.

EVOLUTION OF MATTER.

Now Matter is a state of the One Substance, the all God, but inferior to the other state, Spirit. The all God then is not equally developed. He, therefore, may aspire to the Higher Self and meditate on the time when He shall be all Spirit. He is not then perfect. Hence the development of the inferior state, through evolution, by which the Material Universe, which is the Divine Substance projected into lower conditions, shall attain to the higher.

To support this theory, the homogeneous monads of the Divine Substance are alleged to be incarcerated without individualization in something material. This latter must be God, for all is God. The monads of God are imprisoned in the lower conditions of God, but by whom, is probably one of the mysteries of Occultism.

Who or what starts the process is perhaps another of the mysteries, but when started, it is described as follows in *The Perfect Way:*

"There is no mode of Matter in which the potentiality of personality and therein of man, does not subsist. For every molecule is a mode of the universal consciousness. Without consciousness is no being. The earliest manifestations of consciousness appear in the obedience paid to the laws of gravitation and chemical affinity, which constitute the basis of the later evolved organic laws of nutritive assimilation. And the perception, memory, and experience represented in man are the accumulations of long ages of toil and thought, gradually advancing, through the development of the consciousness, from organic combinations upward to God. Such is the secret meaning of the old mystery-story which relates how Deucalion and Pyrrha, under direction of Themis (wisdom) produced men and women from stones."[6]

"Passing then at length from the mineral Kingdom," says Pember,[7] "the monad is manifested in the lowest modes of organic

---

[6] *The Perfect Way*, p. 19.
[7] *Earth's Earliest Ages*, p. 409.

life, and at this point is individualized by self-generation, and becomes a soul or nucleus to the cell in which it manifested itself." "And once formed, it is capable, on the breaking of its cell, of passing into and informing another cell."[8]

Progress is then made through a series of lives through the vegetable and animal Kingdoms to man.

THE SEPTENARY BEING.

So wonderfully has this process been carried on that man is found to be a "septenary being," for while there are but "four elements which constitute him," according to the *Perfect Way*, *i.e.* the material body, the astral body, the soul or individual, and the Spirit or Divine Father, and life of his system, yet the soul here is a trinity. Thus Judge and Sinnett give man's classification as: (1) The Body, (2) Vitality, (3) Astral Body, (4) Animal Soul, (5) Human Soul, (6) Spiritual Soul and (7) Spirit. The last three form a trinity.

---

[8] *The Perfect Way*, p. 18.

The Spirit or Atma, the Spiritual Soul or Buddhi (being the highest power of intellection, that which discerns and judges) and the Human Soul, the Manas or Mind. This, "the real man," "uses certain agents to get in touch with nature in order to know himself."[9] These are found in the lower four principles in man, the Animal Soul, or the passions and desires, the Life Principle, the Astral Body and the Physical Body. These four material constituents are transitory and subject to separation and disintegration, even as "all the organs of the body are senseless and useless when deprived of the man within."[10]

RE-INCARNATION.

The physical body is absorbed at death into the material elements whence it came forth. The astral body, which can be projected from the material body and made to appear at a distance, is the connecting link

---

[9] See *Ocean of Theosophy*, pp. 32-34.
[10] *Ocean of Theosophy*, p. 34.

between the ethical and the corporeal, and, though it may exist for a while after death and hover over the body, is at length dissipated in and absorbed by the plane of its substance. The life energy does not cease at death but continues its vibrations in the myriad of lives that make up the cells of the body, yet no longer animating them. These four elements belong to the perishable part of man, disappearing at death and reappearing at every new birth. The trinity is the thinker, the individual that passes from one existence to another, gaining experience at each rebirth but advancing or receding according to its deeds in the previous life. In each successive life, one is to others as a new personality but in the complete process he is "one individual conscious of an identity, not dependent on name, form or recollections of personalities." [11]

This is the doctrine of reincarnation, one of the fundamental principles of Theosophy

---

[11] See Article Theosophy by W. Q. Judge in *Johnson's Encyc.*

and necessary to its other scheme of evolution, as there could be no evolution of a human soul without some such idea of transmigration. Connected with these reincarnations is the doctrine of Karma, or justice, whereby they explain the misery and suffering in the world and any national, racial or individual condition is the direct result of the past thoughts or actions of the Egos. The condition of each re-birth is determined by the results of the preceding life according to an inexorable law. The thoroughly evil human souls are finally bereft of the spiritual tie and doomed to annihilation.

NIRVANA.

The pure soul, after many reincarnations, at length rises to the supernatural state, "relinquishes its *existence* for the *being* from which it was originally projected; but returns with conscious individuality and the full advantage of all its experiences. And, returning, it becomes reunited with the Deity, presumably a pure spirit; so that we must conceive of God as a vast spiritual body, constituted of many individual elements all having but one will, and, therefore, being one. This condition of oneness with the Divine Will and Being constitutes what in Hindu mysticism is called the celestial Nirvana."[12] "Though becoming pure spirit, or God, the individual retains his individuality. So that instead of all being finally merged in the One, the One becomes many. God becomes millions."[13] If God be all, and all is God however, what difference does it make? If God is millions, millions are God. Now, that there is no personality to God, is an important doctrine of Theosophy, but millions are God, God is millions, therefore, there is no personality to the millions who have attained to God; if no personality, then no individuality, if no individuality, then nothing but—in fact there is nothing to such existence; and is not Nirvana practically nothingness or annihilation? If so, then after all these processes of

---

[12] *Theosophy*, p. 25.
[13] *The Perfect Way*, p. 19.

reincarnation, with all the troubles and sorrows, the trials and sacrifices of each life, the end, whether you take the regenerate or degenerate course seems to be utter annihilation.

THE FALL.

"The fall of man does not mean .... the lapse .... of particular individuals from a state of perfection. . . . It means such an inversion of the due relations of the soul and body of a personality already both spiritual and material, as involves a transference of the central will of the system concerned from the soul .... to the body, and the consequent subjection of the soul to the body, and liability of the individual to sin, disease and all other evils which result from the limitation of matter."[14] Each individual, of whichever sex, is declared to be a dualism, body and soul, exterior and interior, masculine and feminine—"he the without, she the within." Woman is affirmed to be the proper head of creation, and the subjec-

---

[14] *The Perfect Way*, 215, 186.

tion of the feminine to the masculine in the individual was the Fall, and the outward and visible sign of the Fall is the subjection of woman to man in the world. And it is stated that only by "the complete restoration, crowning and exaltation of the woman, in all planes, that redemption can be effected."[15]

THE ATONEMENT.

Now while the Atonement (at-one-ment) is declared to be the unification of the Body, Soul and Spirit in the individual, continually aspiring to the Divine Spirit, until they constitute one harmonious system under control of the central Will, and redemption consists of a series of acts, spiritual and mental, typified by the six acts of the Lesser and Greater Mysteries, yet the course of human souls, released from their incarcerations in stones, is, that after they have progressed so as to "know the truth," they will be able—whether Jews, Christians, Buddhists, or Mohammedans—to unite in a universal belief of the doc-

---

[15] See *Theosophy*, pp. 414, 415.

trine that *sin* is *expiated* by transmigrations and *in* the *worship* of "the Great Goddess." Probably this is the "twelfth Messiah," and a female, the "Second Eve and the Mother of all Living."

In this system they speak of mind, intelligence, consciousness and will, as attributes of Deity, and yet deny the existence of a Personal God—a manifest contradiction. Possessing these attributes, God must of necessity be a person, but Theosophists are content to simply deny that which controverts their whole theory. But neither have they need of a Saviour. Man can redeem himself and expiate his sin by transmigration. He is made perfect through suffering. "To deprive any one of it by putting the consequences of his acts upon another, so far from aiding one, would be to deprive him of his means of redemption."[16]

KARMA.

There can be no substitution, no pardon, no alleviating circumstances. The conse-

---

[16] *Perfect Way*, 218.

quences of man's thoughts and acts follow just as surely, and in the same ratio, as effect follows cause, according to that inexorable law that govern all things animate and inanimate.

What then is man, according to Theosophy, but a mere passing phase in its process of evolution? As soon as his soul is released from incarceration in the rocks, and he becomes a sentient being, he finds himself subject to inexorable law. This is Karma or Theosophical justice, "the ethical law of causation." It is unchangeable and remorseless. It cannot be set aside. It has to be met and fully satisfied. Prayer then becomes a mockery; your piteous cry in agony for mercy, is simply lost upon the wind; your sincere profession of repentance is utterly powerless to effect the consequences of your act upon yourself; a mistake of judgment counts the same as a deliberate purpose to sin, and so, too, the mother who would relieve her child of the suffering occasioned by accidentally burning its finger would be depriving it of its means of redemption.

This is Karma, "the most important of the laws of nature," "the universal law of harmony," "the twin doctrine to re-incarnation."[17] Your present condition was settled as a consequence of your acts in a previous life, and your acts in the present life will determine your condition when you again become incarnate. You have not the slightest recollection of a previous existence, and so cannot profit by it. You must get as much satisfaction as you can from the fact that, if your condition is one of poverty and obscurity to-day, in a previous existence, of which you have no recollection, you may have been as rich as Crœsus and of royal blood, or that upon the next turn of the cycle you may go up or down according to the unintentional mistakes you may make in this life.

MAHATMAS.

Now on what grounds are we to give up our belief in a Personal God, Who is a merciful and heavenly Father, in a loving Sav-

---

[17] *Ocean of Theosophy*, p. 89.

iour Who redeemed us with His own precious blood, in a sanctifying Spirit Who is the "Lord and Giver of Life," in the ever blessed Trinity who is so marvellously enlightening the world, according as man is enabled to comprehend? Upon what grounds are we to give up the glorious Gospel which has lifted man in the West out of Eastern darkness and misery, which fills him with a progressive spirit, which makes it possible for him to enjoy life here and to be eternally blessed hereafter? Upon what grounds are we to give up the joys, the benefits, the comforts of the religion of Jesus Christ, and turn back to take up with a machine sort of religion which makes man a mere process in the evolution of matter into spirit?

Theosophy says man "has never been without a friend, but has a line of elder brothers, who continually watch over the progress of the less progressive, preserve the knowledge gained through æons of trial and experience, and continually seek for opportunities of drawing the developing intelligence of the race, on this or other globes, to consider the great truths concerning the destiny of the soul."[18] Now these "highly developed men," "perfected from other periods of evolution," are variously called Masters, Adepts, Brothers, Initiates, Mahatmas, meaning great souls—these invisible beings who appear and disappear at will, who travel from place to place with incalculable rapidity—these are they who know all things, who can explain the Mysteries, who told Madame Blavatski all she knew of the Theosophy, who enlightened Col. Olcott, who so inspired the writers of "*The Perfect Way*" that they claim not to be its authors. Yet these "etherealized beings cannot be seen by 'coarse,' 'materialized'" mortals, only by those who have been evolved into the same plane of consciousness.

Of course Theosophy can *in this way* assure us of the truth of its theory; it can explain all things, for the Mahatmas know the truth and understand all the mysteries. They can

---

[18] *Ocean of Theosophy*, p. 3.

explain but do not, because you have not attained to the same plane of consciousness, and so could not comprehend what was communicated. You by chance meet a little boy hurt, disconsolate and crying as if his heart would break. You try to soothe him, and say, "Cheer up, little man; some day you may be President." So Theosophy says to the disconsolate beings of earth, who crave the explanation Theosophy claims to have but does not give: "Cheer up; man is only 18,000,000,000 years old.[19] You are not now on such a plane of consciousness that you can understand. You must be evolved (ground out in this machine) again and again and after one or two million years of such reincarnations, you may become an adept, a Mahatma, and know all things; few ever attain to such heights, but it is possible, even for you. In the meantime, you must be content with what the Mahatmas think you are able to understand, and you are to have implicit faith in it as coming from them.

---

[19] *Ocean of Theosophy*, p. iii. and 18.

The only adepts specifically mentioned are the Asiatic Brotherhood, and they are invisible; too ethereal to communicate with coarse mortals, and need intermediaries; so that you do not get the *ipse dixit* of the Mahatma at first hand but must depend on the assertion of the intermediary.

CLAIMS AND THEIR EXPLANATION.

Theosophists talk of telepathy, mind reading, hypnotism and the alleged astral body which can be projected from the material body. They claim power to influence people separated from them by great distances; give ocular demonstration of their occult powers, and then, if you cannot explain their phenomena, would have you admit the truth of their claims and assertions. Like Spiritualists, they would convince you by ocular demonstration rather than by indisputable testimony which cannot be furnished. Not having such testimony, however, we prefer to explain its phenomena and allegations. We would again refer to the subjective mind. We would see a basis for the theory of an astral body in the double consciousness, a basis for the theory of reincarnations in the fact of life after death. So much then for the modicum of truth underlying the system. As to the invisible Asiatic Brothers flitting around the world in ghostly form and making communications to the select, it is nothing but a scheme advanced to aid in deception. Thus we are not surprised to hear that Mme. Blavatski, the founder of the society, was "an artist in chicanery and a trickster, not only for gain but also for glory."[20] It appears[21] that the Society for Psychical Research investigated the marvellous transportation and duplication of objects and the miraculous conveyance of Mahatma letters. The result was a revelation of trickery. Dishes broken, as if by accident, were picked up, tied in a cloth and put in the Shrine and the door locked. In a few moments the

---

[20] "Mme. Blavatski and Her Dupes," *Current Literature*, Feb., 1898, p. 104.
[21] See same article, *Current Literature*, pp. 105, 106.

dishes were found as good as new. This was said to be done by Mahatmas but it was forgotten to be stated that the accident was premeditated, that the Shrine was connected with Mme. Blavatski's bedroom and that when those dishes were purchased in Madras, duplicates were also procured.

Again, the mortar in one of the interstices between the blocks of wood in a ceiling of a room in a certain house being scraped out, a letter in the well-known handwriting of a Mahatma was inserted and held in place by a thread. When the conversation led up to the proper subject, at a given signal, an accomplice would pull the thread and the letter from Mahatmadom would fall to the floor. By mere accident a package of the Chinese envelopes in which the letters, "actually" conveyed from Thibet, were wont to appear, were found by M. Solovyoff, and Madame Blavatski said to him: "What is one to do, when, in order to rule men, it is necessary to deceive them; when they will not accept even the doctrines of Isis Unveiled without the sanction of miracles; when their very stupidity invites trickery, for almost invariably, the more simple, the more silly, and the more gross the phenomenon, the more likely it is to succeed?"

So it would seem that from the very foundation of the cult, it is surrounded with fraud, trickery and deceit.

BROTHERS, ADEPTS, MAHATMAS—USELESS CREATIONS OF THE IMAGINATION.

The whole scheme of Theosophy, however, with its theories of evolution and re-incarnations, is made to depend on these alleged Mahatmas, the Masters of the Mysteries and communicators of the truth. But who are they? "Highly developed men."[22] But since the world began, there has not been one single authenticated instance of a mortal, in the flesh or out of the flesh, returning from the dead, to communicate with the living and reveal things *known* to *them*, because they have passed into the higher life and see things clearer.

---

[22] *Ocean of Theosophy*, iii.

Passages in the Bible, cited in a previous lecture, prove that when man dies he goes to a definite place, "the place of departed spirits," either Paradise or a "place of torment"; that they are "spirits in prison," *i.e.*, confined, and cannot get back to earth to communicate with the living or to be re-incarnated. There is absolutely no proof of such beings as Mahatmas and consequently no such communication of the alleged truth of Theosophy. If, however, Theosophy can demonstrate anything not hitherto known, it shows that the Eastern religionists have had some insight into the phenomena of the subjective mind of man, long in advance of their brethren of the West, and not yet thoroughly understood. Pember then may be right in saying, "the whole system of the mysteries was communicated by the fallen angels," [23] and with the object of destroying faith in the Lord Jesus and prolonging the reign of the Prince of this world.

---

[23] *Earth's Earliest Ages*, p. 421.

THEOSOPHY VS. CHRISTIANITY.

Look into this evil system of evolution, re-incarnation, fatalism and annihilation, which mystifies rather than instructs, which claims the power to explain all things yet cannot. Compare it with the religion of the glorious Gospel, with all that it has accomplished for the enlightenment and advancement of man, for his peace, his comfort, his happiness, here and hereafter; how it fills him with hope; how, as he lends himself to its influence, it lifts him unto a higher and higher plane of righteousness, purity and sanctity, not in alleged future lives but in this life. And is there a soul who has enjoyed the privileges of living in Christian lands, and who knows of the darkness, wretchedness and slavery of heathenism, that is going to acknowledge the "superiority of ancient sages;" that will relinquish the hope of the Gospel for the inexorable law of Karma or Fatalism; that will turn from the truth, as it is in Jesus, because of the alleged sayings of alleged beings called Mahatmas; that will renounce the Kingdom of Heaven for Nirvana or annihilation; that will refuse henceforth, to offer up on bended knee a prayer to "Our Father, Who art in heaven"; to cry out for pardon unto the Merciful Saviour and to plead for the sanctifying influence of the Holy Spirit, in order to be declared a part of the all God who is being evolved from gross matter to pure spirit?

The old world religions have had their time and proved themselves unable to advance humanity. To what purpose then would you study them? That universal brotherhood is a great way off, if we all have to wait till we are sufficiently evolved, that we can be initiated into the Lodge and become an adept, a brother. Through the inspiring and enlightening influences of the Gospel, we, in the West, are gradually learning more and more of the hidden mysteries or intelligent forces in nature and of the latent powers or psychic forces in man, so that as far as the objects of Theosophy are concerned, it really has no reason for being. We turn from it in disgust, and, falling on bended knee, pray to "Our Father, who art in heaven," to "lighten our minds more and more with the light of the everlasting Gospel," that we may serve Him faithfully in our generation and be gathered to our fathers "having the testimony of a good conscience; in the Communion of the Catholic Church; in the confidence of a certain faith; in the comfort of a reasonable religious and holy hope; in favour with Thee our God and in perfect charity with the world,"[24] through Jesus Christ our Lord.

---

[24] *Prayer Book.*

Christian Science. I.

ITS ORIGIN AND METAPHYSICAL AND THEOLOGICAL TENETS.

FOR some unexplained reason the last quarter of a century seems to be favorable to the attempt to restore the ancient religions and undermine the Gospel of Jesus Christ. So far, then, as their hostility to the Gospel is concerned, Theosophy and Christian Science, which originated about the same time, go hand in hand. Both were given to the world in 1875, and both owe their origin to a woman. Another strange coincidence—Madame Blavatski dabbled in Spiritualism for awhile, but met with an accident in Thibet, being thrown from her horse, and while in a delicate state of health, when one's mind is easily affected, is said to have passed seven years under instruction of Mahatmas and to have emerged in 1875, ready to instruct the world in Theosophy.

Mrs. Eddy, being in poor health in 1862, consulted a distinguished mesmerist, one P. P. Quimby. Later she, too, met with an accident which, according to physicians, must prove fatal. She cured herself, however, before the next noon. She went into retirement, and, after three years, she came to the conclusion that her recovery was in accordance with spiritual laws that could be known and utilized. She then began to teach and write. The result was her great work. *Science and Health* (the 132nd edition of which is before us), was written, but not given to the world till 1875.

NAME.

Mrs. Eddy claims to be the original discoverer of her method of healing, and to have been the first to use the term Christian

Science for this alleged Metaphysical Healing. Now a patent medicine vender, putting a certain nostrum upon the market, gives it whatever name he chooses and has a certain proprietary right to that name, which may in time have a decided marketable value. So Mrs. Eddy is entitled to all the honor and emoluments that may be attached to the name "Christian Science." So far as her theory is concerned, however, we hope, before we get through, to show that she has discovered a subtle force or power in man, the nature of which is not yet well known, but has been used by others, under various names for ages, and that Christian Science itself does not do the healing. When we pause to inquire into the appropriateness of the name given to this method, we find it a misnomer, because it is not Christian and it is not science.

NOT CHRISTIAN.

It is not Christian, for it denies the Christ of history, and invents another. It claims to be founded upon the Holy Scriptures, yet, whenever they controvert any of its tenets, they are twisted and perverted in the effort to assign to them an unnatural and false interpretation. Thus in *Science and Health*, the sole authority for the doctrines of Christian Science according to Mrs. Eddy, its author, a distinction is made between Jesus and the Christ. "Jesus was the Virgin's Son. . . . . Christ is not properly a synonym for Jesus." Evidently Christ is not synonymous but identical with the Holy Ghost, as Mrs. Eddy says: "Throughout all generations, both before and after the Christian era, *the Christ*, as the spiritual idea—as the Holy Ghost, the Comforter—has come, with some measure of power and grace, to all those prepared to receive Him." Again, when "the disciples were first called Christians," it is a common notion that they were so called *after* a *person, not* an *idea*, not even after a "title,"[1] but after the Person to Whom that title "the Christ" belonged. When "the

---

[1] All quotations in this chapter, unless otherwise noted, are from *Science and Health*,

people were in expectation and mused in their hearts of John whether he were the Christ,"[2] they had reference to that Person who was to come to fulfil prophecy. When then Andrew said to Peter: "We have found the Christ,"[3] he brought him to Jesus. But when in response to the question: "Whom say ye that I . . . . am?" Peter declared of Jesus: "Thou art Christ, the Son of the Living God." Mrs. Eddy declares it means: "The Messiah is what thou hast declared—Christ, the divine idea of Truth and Life, which heals mentally."

We have no hesitation in saying that the words bear no such interpretation and that a theory based on such forced and false interpretation of the Word of God cannot be Christian.

NOT A SCIENCE.

As to its claims to be a science, Dr. Jewell well says: "Science reaches truth only through investigation, experiment and

---

[2] S. Luke iii. 15.
[3] S. John i. 41.

discovery—not through revelation."[4] Mrs. Eddy, however, declares God fitted her for "the final revelation of the absolute principle." "Science is classified knowledge, but here is no intelligible classification whatever."[5] "Science aims not only to be exact in its statements but also to set forth . . . logically the truth of its conclusions. But Christian Science appears to rely wholly upon mere assertion, iterated and reiterated without any semblance of close or systematic reasoning;"[6] and finally, as it simmers down to a method of "mind healing," being without classified knowledge in one homogeneous field of truth, it is not a science at all but at best can only claim, like surgery or medicine, to be an art which is "the application of knowledge or skill in effecting a desired result."[7] But under whatever name we investigate it, whether as an art or science, a religion or philosophy, we will find that it cannot stand the test of common sense.

---

[4] *Claims of Christian Science*, p. 14.
[5] *Ibid.* p. 14.   [6] *Ibid.* p. 15.   [7] *Webster.*

FOUNDATION.

Mrs. Eddy, who discovered this Science of Metaphysical Healing in 1866, says: "God had been graciously fitting me, during many years, for the reception of a final revelation of the absolute Principle of Scientific Mind-healing." "No human pen or tongue taught me the Science contained in this book, *Science and Health*, and neither tongue nor pen can overthrow it . . . . the Science and Truth therein will remain forever." "Christian Science is indivisible. There can be but one method of teaching."

Quoting Rev. x. 1, 2, 9, concerning the angel from heaven with "the little book" and the command to eat it, she makes the angel to be "Divine Science which, when understood, is Truth's prism and praise," and "the little book" to be the revelation of Divine Science." Then she declares: "Mortal, obey the heavenly evangel. Take up Divine Science.[8] Read it from beginning to end. Study it, ponder it."

---
[8] At $3.00 per volume.

THE SECOND COMING OF CHRIST.

Again, the discovery of this healing power is declared to be the second coming of Christ, or the second coming of the Gospel of "peace on earth and good will to men."

In her letter, read at the dedication of the Christian Science church in Chicago, last November, Mrs. Eddy refers to a prophecy of Daniel in order to make the same claim.[9]

This seems dangerously near blasphemy in the person who, in the desperate attempt to found her theories upon the eternal verities, alleges that she was "called of God to proclaim His Gospel to this age"; that Christian Science is of "Divine origin"; that Jesus practised according to its rules; that, though He loved mankind, and gave the holy commission to His Apostles to preach and teach, yet He "left no definite rule for demonstrating His Principle of healing and preventing disease," so that it remained unknown until "discovered through Christian Science."

---

[9] See *Chicago Tribune*, Nov. 15, 1897.

I say this is dangerously near blasphemy, so near that, unless its claims can be firmly established, it is blasphemy. But with such plenary inspiration, such marvellous revelation, such sure foundation, such unquestionable sanction, such wonderful "demonstration" as witnessed in the miracles of Jesus, we might reasonably expect to find in Christian Science, called also Divine Science, Spiritual Science, Science of Being, or Science (the terms are interchangeable), the perfection of art, and we are amazed beyond measure that its discoverer could so far forget her "calling" as to declare that she "takes no patients and declines medical consultation."

ITS PHILOSOPHY.

Reserving the consideration of its therapeutics and its popular craze for a subsequent lecture, we turn to examine its philosophy and theology.

The fundamental propositions of Christian Science summarized in the four (to the author) self-evident propositions, are: (1) God is All in all; (2) God is Good, Good is Mind; (3) God, Spirit, being all, nothing is matter; (4) Life, God, omnipotent Good deny death, evil, sin, disease—disease, sin, evil, death deny Good, omnipotent God, Life.

"The metaphysics of Christian Science, like the rules of mathematics, prove the rule by inversion. For example: there is no pain in Truth and no truth in pain; no nerve in Mind and no mind in nerve; no matter in Mind and no mind in matter; no matter in Life and no life in matter; no matter in Good and no good in matter."

BERKELEYISM.

What meaning is intended to be conveyed by the above propositions, what proven, it would be difficult to say. It may be taken as a specimen of the unintelligible character of a most pretentious work but one that is found to be a most illogical, disconnected, bewildering and incomplete conception of the idealism of Bishop Berkeley. Bishop Berkeley, 1685-1753, one of the profoundest thinkers in an age of great men—that of Locke, Swift, Butler, Addison, Pope and others—contended for the unreality of all things outside of his own mind. He was carried to extreme views by his opposition to the materialism and atheism of the time. However, his "system" was neither consistent nor complete but much of it remains sound. In brief, he contended that matter has no independent existence, but is an idea in the supreme mind, which is realized in various forms by the human mind. *Without mind nothing exists.* Cause cannot exist except as it rests in mind and will. All so-called physical causes are merely cases of constant sequence of phenomena. Far from denying the reality of phenomena, Berkeley insists upon it; but contends that reality depends upon the supremacy of mind. *Abstract matter* does *not and cannot* exist. The mind can only perceive qualities of objects, and infers the existence of the objects from them; or, as a modern writer tersely puts it: The only thing certain is mind. Matter is a doubtful and uncertain inference of the human intellect.[10] Mrs. Eddy repudiates the charge that her ideas are borrowed, but when the underlying principle of her system may be tersely expressed in the declaration that "matter is non-existent, mind, and mind alone, exists," we find a striking similarity of ideas. "The 'discovery' of Mrs. Eddy must be limited to the practical application of this principle to human life. She insists that as matter does not exist we should always treat it as non-existent. In this, she is truly original! The few anti-materialistic philosophers have never attempted to carry out this principle."[11]

Concerning this "matter" which is defined as an "illusion" "intelligence . . . . in non-intelligence," "sensation in the sensationless," Mrs. Eddy writes: "Nothing we can say or believe regarding matter is true, except that matter is unreal and is therefore a belief."

THE SENSES.

If we appeal to the senses to controvert this statement, we are met by the declaration that "the material senses cannot bear reliable

---

[10] *World's Best Lit.*, Vol. IX., p. 1804.
[11] *Churchman*, April 11, 1896, p. 490.

testimony." "Any supposed information coming from the body or from inert matter, as if they were intelligent, is an illusion of mortal mind—one of its dreams"—for "Christian Science sustains with immortal proof, the *impossibility of any material sense*, and defines these so-called senses as *mortal beliefs*, whose testimony can neither be true of man or his Maker." "The corporeal senses are the only sources of evil or error. Christian Science shows them to be false; since matter has no sensation, and no organic construction can give it hearing and sight or make it the medium of Mind . . . . A wrong sense of God, man and creation is *non-sense* or want of sense."

We cannot refrain from the declaration that there is much "non-sense" found in Christian Science, which attempts to overthrow the well-nigh universal testimony of mankind that matter does exist and that the evidence of the senses are trustworthy. Yet it is the very object of Christian Science to dispel this error, this belief of mortal mind.

Another object is, to arouse man out of a walking dream. "The history of error is a dream narrative. The dream has no reality, no intelligence, no mind; therefore the dreamer and dream are one; for neither is true or real." "Mortal existence is a dream," and "there is not any more reality in the waking dream of mortal existence than in the sleeping dream." Man then has been compared to one suffering from delirium tremens, everything that he senses is an illusion of mortal mind, but "Mind (immortal mind) must be found superior to all the beliefs of the five corporeal senses and able to destroy all ills." "Sin, sickness and death are to be classified as effects of error." We do not suffer. We think we do, but it is all an error, an illusion. We are not ill. Indeed, "sickness is an illusion to be annihilated by Mind. Disease is an experience of mortal mind."

MIND.

We must, however, distinguish between Mind and mortal mind.

Mind is the "only Principle, Substance, Life, the one God; the only I, the only Us." "The only exterminators of error are the great truths that Good, or God, is the only Mind." "Mind is immortal, and as Mind is never sick, so man cannot be."

"Mortal mind accepts the erroneous material conceptions of life and joy," and is "nothing claiming to be something, an error creating other errors; .... a belief that life substance and intelligence are in and of matter, the subjective states of error," etc., the material senses. "Mind is the grand creator, and there can be no power except that which is derived therefrom." "The struggle for the recovery of invalids goes on, not between material methods but between mortal minds and immortal Mind. The victory will be on the patient's side only as immortal Mind, through Christian Science, subdues the human belief in the disease." Now "mortal mind and body are one. Neither exists without the other. . . . . "Mortal matter, or body, is but a false concept of mortal mind," and is full of mortal belief or error ("a supposition that pleasure and pain—that substance, intelligence, life—are existent in matter"), "and must be changed by immortal Mind," and not by "drugs and hygiene" or any kind of "medication." "Drugs and hygiene oppose the supremacy of the Divine Mind. Drugs and inert matter are unconscious, mindless," and consequently have no power. When the sick recover by the use of drugs, it is the law of general belief, culminating in individual faith, which heals." But of course the drugs, not being themselves real, and their power being an illusion of mortal mind, cannot heal. Metaphysical healing is purely mental. And thus it comes about that, as matter is nonexistent, the material body, which does not exist save as an error of mortal mind (which is nothing, a belief, an error) is led to believe through the senses (which are false and deceptive) that it is afflicted with sickness or disease (which are in turn illusions of mortal mind). Then Christian Science puts forth its power to heal this sickness (which is not a reality), by dispelling the illusion suggested by the false, lying and cheating senses (though they are "impossible") that sickness exists in a material body that does not exist; while the power to heal through Christian Science is demonstrated by means of these same untrue, impossible, corporeal senses.

ITS THEOLOGY.

We turn now to its Theology. God is declared to be Divine Principle, Life, Truth, Spirit, Mind. God is All in all and all is God. "Nothing possesses reality or existence except Mind, God." God is the only Life, the one Spirit. He fills all space, and is "engirdled with the fatherhood and motherhood of Love." As Elias represents the Fatherhood of God through Jesus, so the Revelator (see Rev. XII. 1, 2) completes this figure with woman as the spiritual idea or type of God's Motherhood, and so we find the first petition of the Lord's Prayer blasphemously transposed into: "Our Father and Mother God, all harmonious." This reminds us of Pantheism, and when we are told that man is the compound idea or reflection of God or Mind, and is therefore eternal, that he has no separate mind from God, not a single quality underived from Deity, no life, no intelligence or creative power of his own, but reflects all that belongs to his Maker and co-exists with God and is eternal: and then consider that all reality is Spiritual, we have here a sort of Spiritual Pantheism. As for

THE BLESSED TRINITY.

the Blessed Trinity: "Father is the name for Spirit." "Jesus is the name of the Son of Mary" who "in the flesh (mortal body) was appointed to speak to mortals in such a form of humanity as they could understand as well as perceive," *i.e.*, through corporeal sense, a false faculty and illusion of the mind. "Christ expresses God's spiritual and eternal idea. The name is synonymous (identical) with Messiah and alludes to the spirituality which was taught, illustrated and demonstrated in the life whereof Christ Jesus was the embodiment."

The Holy Ghost, or Spirit, reveals this triune Principle, and is expressed in Divine (Christian) Science which is the Comforter, leading into all Truth.

Now while it must be admitted that these ideas of God and the Blessed Trinity cannot be proven from the Bible, and we know that "all mortals are egotists," yet it seems to reach the height of absurdity to claim that Christian Science is the Comforter.

MAN.

Man is declared to be perfect, as God is perfect, immortal, co-existent with God, "incapable of sin, sickness and death, inasmuch as he derives his essence from God," and is inseparable from Him. "Mortals are man's counterfeits," "material falsities . . . . errors made up of sin, sickness and death, which must give place to the facts which belong to immortal man." Man is not "a material habitation for spirit, but is himself spiritual. . . . . To the senses, man appears to be matter and mind united; but Christian

Science reveals him as the idea of God, and declares the corporeal senses to be mortal and erring illusions."

SOULS.

The term *souls* or *spirits* is as improper as the term gods. Soul or Spirit signifies Deity and nothing else. There is no finite soul or spirit. Those terms mean only one existence." God is All and all is God. God is Spirit, man is spirit, man is God—which is Pantheism. When, then, man is so very spiritual, we are not surprised to learn that "evil is an illusion and error has no real basis." That "the only reality of sin, sickness and death is the awful fact that unrealities seem real to human belief. Sin is identical with sickness and healed in the same way." It is a "species of insanity, *i.e.*, an "hallucination," even as the inmates of asylums are "well defined instances of the baneful effects of illusion on mortal minds and bodies."

Think, if such nonsense can be believed, how wicked it would be to punish a criminal because he is insane; how wrong for the author of *Christian Science* to declare that those who use her "discoveries," without "giving proper credit," are guilty of a "breach of that divine command in the Hebrew decalogue: 'Thou shalt not steal,'" when they were only laboring under an illusion; how shocking it would be to those who in their shameful wickedness break all the commandments of the decalogue, to tell them that evil is an illusion or to reveal to them the "awful" fact that these horrible unrealities seem real to human belief. How quickly they would turn and repent of their evil.

ADAM.

In explaining original sin we get an idea of Christian Science exegesis, for we are told "the word Adam is from the Hebrew, *adamah*, signifying *red*, color of the *ground*, *dust*, *nothingness*. Divide the name Adam into two syllables (two words), and it reads A dam, *i.e.*, an obstruction. This suggests the thought of something fluid, of mortal mind in solution, of the darkness which seemed to appear when 'darkness was upon the face of the deep,' and matter stood as opposed to Spirit, as that which is accursed. Jehovah declared the ground—matter—accursed; and from this earth, or matter, sprang Adam, although God had blessed the earth 'for man's sake.' From this, it follows that Adam was not the ideal man for whom the earth was blessed." Adam then stands for "error; a falsity; evil; a curse; nothingness; the belief in original sin." Was ever greater ignorance and absurdity combined in a single argument!

ANTI-CHRISTIAN.

We are not surprised that a system that denies the unreality of the senses and all things material, would declare the Scriptural account of creation as recorded in Genesis to be "allegorical" and prefer an alleged spiritual rather than literal interpretation of the Word of God. But when, though speaking kindly of the Lord Jesus, this system would attempt to deprive Him of His Divine

Sonship and Equality with the Father Almighty; has no need of Him as Saviour of mankind; would take away as unnecessary His pardoning power; would destroy His atonement; would controvert His vicarious sacrifice; would change the idea of Baptism; would declare the institution of the Blessed Sacrament "foolish in a literal sense," and that if Christ, Truth, is Immanuel, God with us, no commemoration is necessary, notwithstanding the words: "Do this in remembrance of Me;" when it declares that man has the same body after death as before, and that he is immortal, and so men do not have to come to Christ Jesus "that they may have life," and that He may "raise them up at the last day"—whatever we may think of the members thereof, the system is decidedly anti-Christian. It is illogical, inconsistent, unreasonable. It cannot stand the test of common sense. It cannot stand alone, and so it bolsters itself up on the Blessed Gospel of Jesus the Christ to which it is as false as false can be.

But, then, we know that the testimony of our senses can be relied upon.

We know that matter is real.

We know, when our conscience convinces us of sin, that sin is there; it is no illusion.

We know with S. John that "If we say we have no sin we deceive ourselves and the truth is not in us."

We know that this whole system, which is against our own senses and our personal experience of life, is wrong from beginning to end.

We know too what the Prayer Book says: That we may "be made like unto Christ by suffering patiently adversities, troubles, sicknesses. For He Himself went not up to joy before He suffered pain; He entered not into His glory, before He was crucified. So, truly, our way to eternal joy is to suffering here with Christ."[12] And the sufferings of our Saviour have moved more men to repentance and reformation than all other moral forces combined, and, more than

---

[12] *Prayer Book Visitation of the Sick.*

all others, have deepened throughout the world the sense of the infinite preciousness of personal goodness. And the explanation of this power must be sought in the constitution of the universe and in the nature of man himself. As Horace Bushnell has masterfully depicted the very universe itself in vicarious sacrifice:

> " Life evermore is fed by death,
>   In earth and sea and sky;
> And that a rose may breathe its breath
>   Something must die."[13]

[13] *Argument for Christianity*, p. 270-271.

Christian Science. II.

ITS THERAPEUTICS.

CHRISTIAN SCIENCE claims to be the science of metaphysical healing. We admit it to be an art. As an art of healing, then, what has it done? What can it do? That pain has been alleviated, that some diseases have been cured by Scientists, we are willing to concede. We however defy anyone to prove that such "healing" is due to that illogical, self-contradictory, "non-sensical," anti-Christian conglomeration, falsely called Christian Science.

THE DISCOVERY.

What the author of *Health and Science* "discovered" is a principle of human nature (yet to be proven most valuable and useful) which makes possible the actual cures of all these healers of whatever sort, which was "discovered" and made use of by soothsayers and magi and all that class in the East, long before the Christian era. Not knowing what this principle is, one and all of these healers claim it to be a proof of their respective theory and the power that they possess. Not knowing the scope of its powers or the laws by which it is governed, it becomes a dangerous force, however, in the hands of the many modern demonstrators, and for the safety of humanity (especially of children) they should be held liable for every death *due to the ignorant use of this power.*

THE VIS MEDICATRIX NATURÆ.

In considering the art of healing in general, we must take into account, as a most important element, what is called the *Vis Medicatrix Naturæ*, the healing or recuperative power of nature. Disease, you know, is an abnormal condition and nature is endowed with a power to restore our bodies to their tnormal state. It is, as we well know, not always able to do this, being at times too completely obstructed; and so it is the province of the learned physician, not to perform marvellous cures—he does not cure—but to exercise his skill in assisting nature by counteracting, nullifying or removing whatsoever hinders its wonderful recuperative efforts. Of this ever active and assertive power of nature, Sir John Marshall, F.R.S., said: "The *Vis Medicatrix Naturæ* is the agent to employ in the healing of an ulcer or the union of a broken bone; and it is equally true that the physician or surgeon never cures a disease; he only assists the natural processes of cure performed by the intrinsic conservative energy of the frame, and this is but the extension of the force imparted at the origination of the individual being."[1]

Thus we may understand how one may be restored to health in spite of malpractice and why good nursing is so heartily commended by physicians; in the one instance, the won-

---

[1] Buckley. *Faith Healing—Christian Science*, p. 277.

derful recuperative power of nature has succeeded in spite of the ignorance of the practitioner; and in the other, the nursing assisted nature in a recovery that was made certain and more speedy by its aid.

THE INFLUENCE OF THE MIND.

It is well known that the dominant mental state has a wholesome or depressing effect upon the organs of the body, so that many of the ills of which people complain, being imaginary, they may be dispelled by a complete and radical change of one's mental condition. "Mental impressions, however produced, it is said, act through the nervous system upon the organs of the body, so as to stimulate or to obstruct their functions. Thus, fright, grief, hope, cheerfulness, determination to get well, or despair, all register themselves in the bodily condition."[2]

How often have we heard of people said to have frightened themselves into sickness. Caring for the sick, they have in fear conceived

---
[2] See Shinn's *Modern Substitutes for Christianity*, p. 46.

the idea that they have contracted the same disease. How often through despair and sometimes nothing but sheer laziness, people neglect the body until they become morose, despondent, morbid. They have innumerable aches and pains and require constant attendance, medical and otherwise. Here then is a field for marvellous cures by bread pills, colored water, faith, Christian Science, mesmerism, spiritualism and every kind of healing art. Whatever the means employed, however, the underlying fact is that through hope, faith, a desire to get well, through finding a purpose in life, by being given something to do, through imparted cheerfulness, the mind is roused out of its morbid condition, everything around one again becomes bright, he is filled with hope and expectancy and in consequence, the sluggish organs of the body are so stimulated to activity that all symptoms of the imaginary disease vanish away.

CHARLATANRY.

Victims of charlatanry are found in the cases of those who, after severe sickness or dangerous accident, are persuaded (in their own minds) that they are hopeless invalids. In illustration, there comes to my mind the instance of a lady who, recovering from a terrible accident, thought that she could never walk again. Her physician declared that there was no reason why she could not walk and at his suggestion, she was left in her arm chair under a tree, one summer afternoon, when a thunderstorm was approaching. She was always much alarmed by such storms and when she found that she was forgotten or neglected, she declared she got up and walked into the house and has walked ever since. What a marvellous cure this might have proven, if she had fallen into the hands of a healer, while still under her hallucination. Still other cases for the charlatan are those where the patient has passed the crisis and nothing remains to be done but with careful nursing to wait for nature to complete the restoration to health. Often, however, this does not take place as rapidly as desired (due frequently to ignorance and improper care) and so a change of physicians is made or one of the many kinds of healers is called in, and to the latter is given the undeserved, unearned credit of bringing about the recovery.

ACTUAL CURES.

It is admitted, however, that some cures by Christian Science healers and others are genuine, but it is firmly maintained that they pertain to functional, not organic diseases, that is, to those diseases the symptoms of which cannot be referred to any appreciable change of structure or derangement of an organ, and not to those attended with morbid changes of the structure of the organs of the body or in the composition of its fluids; or again, to ailments due to "nerval derangement" and not to those due to the invasion of microbes.

PERCENTAGE OF CURES. THE PRINCIPLE.

Furthermore, it is alleged that five per cent. of those who went to the healer Schlatter were cured. Five per cent. also of those incurables who take "The White Train" in France to visit the Grotto of Lourdes and who are examined by physicians before and after going, are pronounced cured. Christian Science, it is said, takes no account of its failures. We may therefore place its percentage on a level with those others, for whether we consider the cures of Christian Science, of Schlatter, of Lourdes or other wonder-working shrines, of faith, of mind cures, of mesmerism, of spiritualism, of magnetic healers, of Indian medicine men, of Hindoo Yogis, of Egyptian Fakirs or of the old Eastern soothsayers before the Christian era, the principle is identical in one and all and so is not only no new "discovery" of this age but is even independent of all these systems, Christian Science as well as all the others, that it is alleged to support. That principle is the same that the fond mother makes use of when, her little child crying with the pain from a burned finger, she gives her a new doll and causes her to forget all about the pain.

Grasp this principle and you can explain all these marvellous cures.

THE PRINCIPLE.

Let us attempt to get an insight into it.

I.—PAINLESSNESS—A FREAK OF NATURE.

It is narrated of one Miss Evatima Tardo, who was born on the island of Trinidad, West Indies, and is now 26 years of age, that she does not know pain and has never had any feeling or sense of touch. It is said to be due to a defect in her nervous system. Snakes bite her, pins are thrust into her body, through her cheek; flesh wounds are made by knife or pistol ball, and she feels no pain. The wounds are not denied, because they do not pain. They are plainly to be seen. They heal very rapidly, however, because of the absence of pain or feeling which in ordinary mortals delays the recuperative powers of nature. Miss Tardo can also control the circulation of her blood, when bitten by a snake, allowing the wound to bleed or not, at will.[3]

---

[3] See Minneapolis *Journal*, Aug. 10 and 14, '97; New York *Sunday World*, Aug., '97, also *Tid Bits*, Dec., '97.

II. PAINLESSNESS; SUPERCONSCIOUSNESS OR CONTROL OF THE SENSES.

From Miss Tardo, we go to the Hindoo lecturer on Vedanta philosophy, in this country, Swami Abhedananda, who in an interview in the *Sun*[4] (N. Y., Dec. 26, 1897) said concerning our blessed Lord, that, having (in Gethsemane) "reached the state of mind known to Hindus as samahdi or superconsciousness," "there was no pain for Him on the cross; that the nails driven into His hands and feet excited no more sensibility than they would, if driven into so much wood." He then explained what was "meant by the control of the senses as illustrated in the case of Christ." He tells of a sage, Chaitanga, who was tested for the control of his senses, by holding some powdered sugar on his tongue for ten minutes and then blowing it off as dry as ever. Again he tells of another sage in India. Outside of the city, robbers had taken him for a spy and chopped off his right arm. He quickly walked back to the

---

[4] See *Literary Digest*, Jan. 15, 1898, p. 81.

city. A kind-hearted Brahmin met him, recognized him and fell at his feet, binding up his wound. But the sage was hardly aware that he had been wounded. "His countenance glowed with deep calmness and tranquillity. He had not only withdrawn his senses but he had shut his soul entirely in from his mind." Other sages have been chopped to pieces uttering the declaration all the while that they "could not be killed." Still again, he tells of a friend of his in London going to see a Spaniard who claimed to have entire control of his senses. Submitting to a test, a doctor drove a needle between the nail and flesh of his thumb. The Spaniard did not wince but went on laughing and talking to his friends. After some minutes, he was requested to relax his mind. Of course when he did so, he was seized with the most excruciating pain and blood began to run from the wound. "It is by such concentration of mind," he declares, "that one is able to separate the soul from the mind and free it from the knowledge of matter."

These examples show us the possibility of the absence of pain or of a state of unconsciousness of both pain and suffering, and that this state of unconsciousness can be brought about through the control of the senses. It also shows within man something that can control the senses. What is this something?

III. THE SUBJECTIVE MIND.

The Very Reverend Dean Hart, in his examination of Christian Science says: "It is now beginning to be recognized that the human mind is not one uniform and homogeneous machine; it contains wheels within wheels. To the close observer, it becomes evident that parts of the mind are capable of almost independent action. It is a common experience with men who are accustomed to speaking in public, that they are conscious of two currents of thought; the lips pronouncing one, and the other part of the mind preparing for what is coming next, or probably making some observation connected with their audience, which shall modify their mode of address. We seem to be aiming at the conclusion that beneath the active surface of the mind, there lies an inactive but recipient mental plane which has been called the subjective mind."[5]

That this subjective mind does exist, that it receives impressions and retains them, he declares, is frequently "evidenced in the sudden recollection of a series of events absolutely forgotten" and again by the "common occurrence with persons on the brink of sudden death, when the events of their entire life pass before their mental view in rapid panorama."

Swami Abhedananda, the Hindu lecturer to whom we have referred before, declares further that by "concentration of mind, the soul is departed from the mind and freed from bondage to matter."[6] He further says that "according to the Vedanta view of Christ, all of us will some day . . . .

---

[5] *A Way that Seemeth Right*, pp. 46–47.
[6] *Lit. Digest*, Jan. 15, 1898, p. 81.

become Christ, for in every one of us is the pure and sublime soul that shows forth from Him on the Mount of Transfiguration. It needs only to be set free, to connect itself with this cosmic intelligence that stands behind and directs, evolves and projects all these forms of matter that we see."[7] Then he asks: "What do we see in ourselves? First, the body, then behind it the mind, and behind that something that is conscious of them both. One can often separate all three of them in such a manner as to see their difference. This soul or cosmic consciousness behind everything, is able to manifest itself in man more freely than in anything else, because of the more nearly perfect form of his mind and body."[8]

THE DOUBLE EGO OR DOUBLED CONSCIOUSNESS.

We turn from this Hindu then, with his idea of "concentration of mind," something behind both mind and body, this supercon-

---

[7] *Lit. Digest*, Jan. 15, 1898, p. 80.
[8] *Ibid.* pp. 80–82.

scious state and from the subjective mind, to the theory of the psychologist, Max Dessoir, of Berlin, concerning the "Doppel Ich," or, Double Ego. He supposes that human personality is a unity merely to our consciousness, but that it consists really of at least two clearly distinguishable personalities, each held together by its own chain of memories.[9]

[An illustration is given in the case of one Barkworth, adding up a long row of figures at the same time that he carried on a lively conversation.] His idea is that there is an unconscious intelligence in man and an unconscious memory, and that as consciousness and memory are the two elements of personality, he concludes that there must be a second personality. The mental processes which tak place consciously to the man (says Moll), are called the primary consciousness, and those which go on without his knowledge the secondary consciousness; the action of both together is a state of double consciousness, or doubled consciousness.[10] Two

---

[9] Moll's *Hypnotism*, p. 259.   [10] *Ibid.* p. 260.

entirely separate personalities in an individual, as though A carried within himself the personality of B is not to be supposed. The Double Ego is not to be so conceived, but is only a diagram to indicate the fact that psychic processes may go on within us, unobserved, and often yielding no evidence of themselves except their results."[11]

IV. HYPNOTIC SUGGESTION.

We turn now to hypnosis, and the peculiar state into which subjects are thrown by bringing into play this secondary consciousness. This is entirely a subjective state, by which control is obtained of the physical functions and sensations. Thus the Aïssaouas of Constantine, Algiers, are able by means of dancing and singing to throw themselves into a state of ecstacy, difficult to describe, in which their bodies seem insensible even to severe wounds. They run pointed iron into their heads, eyes, neck and breasts without

---

[11] Moll's *Hypnotism*, p. 260.

injuring themselves. Behold how the senses may be controlled and by what means.[12]

Now let us understand that this secondary consciousness, which plays so important a part, which Dessoir calls: " The hidden half of our mental life;"[13] which evidently itself brings into subjection the physical functions and sensations, is always amenable to suggestion, whether it be external or autosuggestion. By suggestion, Moll[14] has reference to the commands given to subjects, the promptings and persuasions used to influence them. The clearest definition of suggestion is to be found in the Century Dictionary, namely, "The insinuation of a belief or impulse into the mind of the subject by any means, as by words or gestures, usually by emphatic declaration; also the impulse of trust which leads to the effectiveness of such incitement;" while suggestibility is defined as "the impression on the mind of an idea,

---

[12] Moll's *Hypnotism*, p. 42.
[13] *Ibid*. p. 261.
[14] *Ibid*. p. 36.

image, movement, which the person reproduces voluntarily or involuntarily."[15]

Now let us take an example of a healing by suggestion.[16] We wish to cure a headache by arousing in the subject the idea that the headache is gone. Spontaneous reflection would prevent this in most waking people, but in hypnosis ideas are more easily established. If the subject accepts the suggestion, we may be sure that, in the hypnotic state, he does not feel the pain. But now we have to prevent the pain after waking. Either external post-hypnotic suggestion or auto-suggestion will do this. We can make the patient continue to think the pain is gone after he wakes. He need not be conscious of this idea, in the sense of remembering it. On the contrary, the less conscious the idea is, the more effect it will have, because reflection will not struggle against it. Auto-suggestion is the second plan. The patient, finding himself without pain in hypnosis, may convince

---

[15] See Wolcott's *What is Christian Science*, p. 58.
[16] Moll's *Hypnotism*, p. 346.

himself that pain is not a necessary consequence of his state, and this idea may under some circumstances be strong enough to prevent the return of the pain.[17]

Furthermore, suggestibility sometimes exists where there is not evidence that the subject is in the hypnotic state. Dean Hart, in the work before quoted, narrates from the *British Foreign Medical Review*, a case reported by a naval surgeon as follows: "A very intelligent officer had suffered for some years from violent attacks of cramps in the stomach. These attacks came on monthly, or oftener, and subnitrate of bismuth had been used with good results, but, notwithstanding that the dose was increased to the largest extent that its poisonous qualities would justify, it lost its effects. Sedatives were again used, but while suffering greatly rom the effects of some preparation of opiumf he was told that on the next attack he would be put under the effect of a medicine which was generally believed to be most effective,

---

[17] Moll's *Hypnotism*, pp. 346, 347.

but which was rarely used because of its dangerous qualities; but that, notwithstanding these, it would be tried, provided he gave his consent. This he did willingly. Accordingly, on the first attack after this, a powder containing four grains of *ground biscuit* was administered every seven minutes, while the greatest anxiety was expressed (within the hearing of the patient) lest too much should be given. The fourth dose caused an entire cessation of pain. Half drachm doses of bismuth had never produced the same relief in less than three hours. Four times the same remedy was used however with the same result. After that he left the ship."[18] This leads the Dean to declare that "thought of any given bodily change tends to the actual production in the body of the change that thought suggests."

EXPLANATION OF THE CURES.

We are now in a condition to explain the marvellous cures of functional or even organic diseases whether by Schlatter, the medicine

---

[18] *A Way That Seemeth Right*, pp. 22, 23, 24.

man of the Indians, the mesmeric healer, faith healer, spiritualist, Hindu Yogi, Eastern fakir or Christian Scientist. The principle is one, if the methods vary. With the scientist the patient (subject) is regarded as laboring under a delusion, an illusion, is told that he is not sick, that he has no pain and that he should act accordingly (*i.e.*, as a well person.) Here is the suggestion. (If the subject is not actually hypnotized he is under the influence of hypnotic suggestion.) The tendency is to produce in the body the change that thought suggests.

More than this, the suggestion arouses the secondary consciousness, that mighty something within us that controls our sensations and (the senses under abeyance) the body is not racked with pain; in consequence the healing process goes on more rapidly. Then take into account the fact that the mighty recuperative force of nature (the *vis medicatrix naturæ*,) always at work, must act more rapidly and successfully under these favorable circumstances, and we see why the patient may recover without the use of medicine.

EXCEPTIONS.

Whensoever these marvellous cures are made then, this is the principle, but it does not always act. In many cases it should not be attempted. Unfortunately for Christian Science, it only makes one exception. It advises that "adjustment of broken bones and dislocations" be left to the fingers of a surgeon, saying, "Christian Science is always the most skilful surgeon, but surgery is the branch of its healing which will be last demonstrated."

ITS HARMFULNESS.

As Christian Science makes no other exceptions, its healers who presume to give treatment to the afflicted are an actual menace to a community, because they condemn every other kind of treatment; because they do not presume to diagnose a case; because they spurn anatomy and physiology; because they are grossly ignorant of the power that they possess. We admit in some instances this treatment is successful, but we also declare, that in certain kinds of diseases it is worse than useless to attempt it, as is well known to those who understand what this power is by which such healing is brought about. Being incapable of telling when to use it and when not to use it, and so using it indiscriminately, these so-called healers become dangerous, a menace to the community. If after having tried it and found it a miserable failure (not because it is useless, but because its power is abused through ignorance) they would then admit such failure and call in a physician before it is too late, it would not be quite so dangerous. But even so, they should not be allowed to practise it, any more than a child should be allowed to play with a razor. If they do practice and a patient dies through their criminal ignorance and negligence, why should they not be held for malpractice the same as any other practitioner? Again, if this science is "divine," if Jesus Christ practised according to its rules, if He taught

His "students" (disciples) the generalities of this principle as claimed, yet they, like the Master, administered to the afflicted without money and without price. But the students of the author who claimed to be "called of God to proclaim His Gospel to this age," i.e., through her book, *Science and Health*, turn their treatment to pecuniary benefit and so would seem to put themselves in the class with Simon the sorcerer, who would traffic with the gift of God and was so severely rebuked by St. Peter. [19]

CONCLUSION.

We have earnestly and honestly tried to ascertain what there is in the alleged healing power of Christian Science, so called. We have found a principle of action, a principle within man, long used in the East, of more recent discovery in the West, yet bound to be more thoroughly known, which is no more peculiar to Christian Science than to any other of the many mysterious modes of heal-

---

[19] *Acts* viii; 18-20.

ing. That principle is of benefit in some kinds of ailments and will be found of more use, when it is more thoroughly understood. The principle will remain when the theory of Christian Science is forgotten. As a theory, it is ill conceived, illogical and in some places utterly senseless. But, above all, while claiming to be Christian and to be based upon the Bible, it is decidedly anti-Christian even as its doctrines will be found to be contrary to the truth as it is in Jesus.

Conclusion.

THE REASON AND THE REMEDY FOR THESE ANTI-CHRISTIAN CULTS.

IN the consideration of some modern substitutes for the Gospel or anti-Christian cults, we tried to ascertain what there was in Spiritualism, Theosophy and Christian Science. We found that it was an historical fact that during the last quarter of a century there is ever an attempt made to restore the ancient religions. Spiritualism we know was practised in some of its many forms from the earliest ages in the history of man.

Theosophy affirms and declares that we should study the ancient religions and "confess to the superiority of the ancient sages."

Christian Science, as a healing art, we discovered, rests upon the same principle as that which governed the cures of Eastern soothsayers and fakirs long before the Christian era. We can, with reason, then, ascribe their prominence to-day to that peculiar epidemic that characterizes the last quarter of a century, which is decidedly as anti-Christian, as they are.

SPIRITUALISM.

We found Spiritualism to be so surrounded with fraud, trickery and deceit that it was difficult to find even the modicum of truth necessary to give it any hold upon an intelligent and not a superstitious people. We found its marvellous manifestations and phenomena could all be duplicated by the honest presdigitateur, through his own skill, and, therefore, that it was needless to call in the aid of unseen, disembodied spirits. As for these alleged communications with the spirits of the departed, we learned from the Bible that the spirits of the departed are held in abeyance, confined, imprisoned in some place from which they cannot return, and that it is doubtful if they are conscious of what is going on in the carnal world. Wherefore, we conclude that whatever marvellous powers they seem to have are due to mind-reading, telepathy, hypnotism, or some other phenomena of the subjective mind, which phenomena, known and made use of in the East for centuries, may have been revealed to them by the evil spirits that inhabit the air and in the interest of the Prince of this world, whose limited reign seems to be at its height.

Spiritualism, in principle, is in defiance of Almighty God, in claiming to reveal that which He does not purpose to reveal. It has no need of a Saviour; it looks forward to a female Messiah, and, contrary to the teaching of the Bible that, "now is the accepted time," teaches that our sins can be atoned for hereafter.

THEOSOPHY.

Theosophy is a system evolved out of a combination of the doctrines of evolution, reincarnation, fatalism and Pantheism. It is admittedly pagan in its origin and claims its occultism to be "handed down from the times of the Mysteries to the present." It cannot admit a personal God, and says the "Father in Heaven is a well known esoteric phase for the Higher Self," but God is all and all is God. It starts with Substance, God, Living Substance, which has two states: the higher spirit and that which is projected into lower conditions, matter. Both, of course, are eternal and the process we see going on in the world is the evolution of matter into spirit.

Man is not a creature of God, but a result in the development of this process; and he came forth from the rocks. His present state is the result of what he did in a previous life, of which he has no memory or consciousness, and his condition, when next he becomes incarnate, depends upon what he does in this stage of his existence—the king may become the bootblack, the washerwoman, the literateur. So it goes on through the countless ages, up or down, till by regeneration or degeneration man attains to annihilation.

Pain and suffering, misery and happiness are results of what one has done in previous existence, following the rule of cause and effect and to relieve one of his distress is to interfere with his redemption. Consequently there is no mercy, no pardon, no vicarious sacrifice, no Saviour, only the stern hard road of fate. With woman declared to be the head of creation, the outward and visible sign of the Fall is the subjection of woman to man in the world, and her complete restoration and exaltation is necessary before redemption can be effected; while the progress in the development of souls will lead to the "universal belief of the doctrine that sin is expiated by transmigrations and in the worship of the Great Goddess."

The Holy Spirit is looked upon as the female element in the Divine Substance and Christ is declared to be a title given to all triumphant Initiates, of which there have been eleven, and another is yet to come to reconcile the seeming differences of his predecessors and to acknowledge the Christs of all nations.

CONCLUSION.

Of course, Theosophy would reduce Christianity to the level of the ancient religions, that, out of all, it might be acknowledged the universal religion. It does not directly attack the Bible and its doctrines but it would explain them so as to advance its own cause.

It rests its theories upon the revelation of a line of elder brothers, Christs, Mahatmas, Adepts, Initiates, "highly developed men," "perfected forms of other periods of evolution," invisible beings of whom great things are claimed, who are alleged to have told Mme. Blavatski and other leaders all they knew of this mysterious system; but there is not the slightest evidence that such beings exist. Indeed, the Bible would teach that those who have passed from this earth cannot return or communicate with its inhabitants.

Theosophy condemns the trickery of Spiritualism yet is not itself free from this same means used to advance its cause, but there are none of its phenomena, that are genuine, that cannot be explained through the secondary consciousness made use of by ancient sages of the East, but not known till recent years in the West.

CHRISTIAN SCIENCE.

Christian Science we found to be the name given to a theory woven around an alleged discovery of an art of healing, the principle of which, however, has been made use of by all kinds of healers, ancient as well as modern. The explanation is found in the secondary consciousness of man, responding to hypnotic suggestion. Cures are performed in this way assuredly, but there is a most decided limit and it is worse than useless to apply it in all cases. As this is attempted, however, and lives are actually lost in this way, it becomes a dangerous principle in the hands of ignorant healers and should be restricted.

As a theory, it is the idealism of Bishop Berkeley, attempted to be put into practical every day life. Declaring matter non-existent and nothing real but mind or spirit, it would counteract, heal, the evil effects, which active nothingness (sin, sickness and death) exerts upon the lives of men but which it declares to be illusions of mortal mind.

As a science, it is a misnomer, illogical, incomplete, inconsistent and altogether untrustworthy. As a religion, it is anti-Christian. It twists, perverts and contradicts the plain teaching of the Bible and denies the Christ of history to advance its own untenable assertions. If ever there was an illusion, it is what is called Christian Science, which raises a hope in the breasts of its adherents which they will find, when too late, that it is utterly incapable of satisfying.

But why will people follow after such things? Why should we desire to peer into the future when our own experience teaches us that it is best for us not to know what is in store for us? Why should we desire to explain all things (with the Theosophists) when we know that it is impossible, or what satisfaction can it be when we are suffering and in want, while others rejoice and have abundance, to know that it is according to the law of Karma and due to something done in a previous existence? Why should we desire to deny the testimony of the senses? Why deny the reality of pain and suffering?

We know that this is not a perfect world and that in the midst of its joys and happiness, trouble, toil and pain are sure to come; but we also know that sorrow has its uses and that by reason of the crosses, often grievous that we have had to bear, we have grown purer, nobler, better, happier, so that, though it meant agony to us at the time, we have cause to rejoice that we were made to go through the fiery furnace of affliction.

THE REASON.

Why then do men to-day take up with these substitutes for the Gospel instead of taking up their cross to follow Jesus? The reason is plain. They have not learned that "there is none other Name under heaven given among men, whereby we must be saved."

They have not yet acknowledged that the only true religion is the Gospel, the only true hope of salvation that of Jesus of Nazareth. When then they see so many of the household of faith cold, indifferent, listless believers, having the form of Godliness but denying the power thereof, believing in spite of themselves, yet finding no hope and joy and comfort in believing—when they see Christendom divided up into a multitude of sects, caring not so much for the cause of the Master, as for their own sect, unable perhaps to repeat the "Faith once for all delivered to the saints" and "contending earnestly" for their own opinions rather than for that—when this condition of things is recognized as existing among those who profess and call themselves Christians, it is not strange that the world should look askance or that others should at times be inclined to advance ideas of their own, even if they are not distinctly Christian. And, it must be admitted, just as soon as we depart a single iota from the "Faith once for all delivered" one individual or organization has as much right to advance his ideas and opinion as another, whether Christian or not. It must also be admitted that it is not pleasant to think that we are responsible beings held to account for all that is done in the flesh or that there is but one way of salvation, one way to obtain immortal life. With the responsibility of eternity before us, it is not pleasant to think of the uncertainty of the future; or that we must suffer while others know nought but joy; or that our trials and troubles are all needless. When therefore theories are advanced that would relieve us of such things, it is not strange that there are some poor souls that are attracted by them. But 'tis all in vain; God's plans for the salvation of mankind are not to be overthrown by man's connivance. We poor mortals are to walk by faith, not by knowledge; and when trials and tribulations come upon us, as must needs be, our hope, our comfort, is to be found not in denying them but in waiting upon the Lord and hearing Him say to us as to S. Paul: "My grace is sufficient for thee; for my strength is made perfect in weakness." This is the panacea of all earthly ills, which will enable us, not to deny or ignore them but to triumph over them.

THE REMEDY.

If then we have found the cause of these ills, for so they really are, have we not also found the cure, the remedy, in a complete trust in an active living faith in the Lord Jesus, that would lead us to proclaim from the housetop if need be, but much better in an holy Christian living, that there is none other name under heaven given among men whereby we may receive health and salvation but only the name of our Lord Jesus Christ!

Oh, then that we knew more about the Church of the living God, what it is, what it claims and what it stands for! Oh, that we could realize the mighty power of the Gospel of Jesus Christ; not so much in the past as in the present; not so much by what it has done as by what it can do for us here and now!

Oh, that we might realize the power of Jesus Christ over mankind and in ourselves. Then would we no longer seek in vain to flee the uncertainties, the sorrows, the pain, the anguish to be found in this temporal world, for the Cross and the abundant grace given, would enable us to triumph over them, to rejoice in spite of them—yea, conquerors through our great Redeemer's might, sealed with His eternal Name, we shall find perfect health and eternal salvation, and it may be sung of us as of the Saints in Light:

"Hunger, thirst, disease unknown,
On immortal fruits they feed;
Them the Lamb amidst the throne,
Shall to living fountains lead.

"Joy and gladness banish sighs;
Perfect love dispels their fears;
And forever from their eyes,
God shall wipe away their tears."

THE END.

www.ingramcontent.com/pod-product-compliance
Lightning Source LLC
Chambersburg PA
CBHW020309170426
43202CB00008B/553